7 Wonders of the World

The History and Legacy of the Ancient Greek City

(Getting Us More Attracted to the Creations and Wonders of the World)

Debra Ladner

Published By **Andrew Zen**

Debra Ladner

All Rights Reserved

7 Wonders of the World: The History and Legacy of the Ancient Greek City (Getting Us More Attracted to the Creations and Wonders of the World)

ISBN 978-1-77485-695-6

No part of this guidebook shall be reproduced in any form without permission in writing from the publisher except in the case of brief quotations embodied in critical articles or reviews.

Legal & Disclaimer

The information contained in this ebook is not designed to replace or take the place of any form of medicine or professional medical advice. The information in this ebook has been provided for educational & entertainment purposes only.

The information contained in this book has been compiled from sources deemed reliable, and it is accurate to the best of the Author's knowledge; however, the Author cannot guarantee its accuracy and validity and cannot be held liable for any errors or omissions. Changes are periodically made to this book. You must consult your doctor or get professional medical advice before using any of the suggested remedies, techniques, or information in this book.

Upon using the information contained in this book, you agree to hold harmless the Author from and against any damages, costs, and expenses, including any legal fees potentially resulting from the application of any of the information provided by this guide. This disclaimer applies to any damages or injury caused by the use and application, whether directly or indirectly, of any advice or information presented, whether for breach of contract, tort, negligence, personal injury, criminal intent, or under any other cause of action.

You agree to accept all risks of using the information presented inside this book. You need to consult a professional medical practitioner in order to ensure you are both able and healthy enough to participate in this program.

TABLE OF CONTENTS

Introduction 1

Chapter 1: The Great Pyramid Of Giza 2

Chapter 2: The Hanging Garden Of Babylon 7

Chapter 3: The Temple Of Artemis 20

Chapter 4: The Statue Of Zeus At Olympia 30

Chapter 5: Colossus Of Rhodes 38

Chapter 6: Light House Of Alexandria 44

Chapter 7: Mausoleum At Halicarnassus 49

Chapter 8: Compiling A List Of Wonders 54

Chapter 9: The Superstructure 122

Conclusion 184

Introduction

This book consist of an information for Tourist purposes and educational reasons and contents as thus-There were Seven Wonders of the Ancient World which refers to remarkable constructions of classical antiquities listed in this book popular among the ancient Greek tourists, particularly in the 1st and 2nd centuries BC. The most renowned of these, the versions by Antipater of Sidon and an observer identified as Philon of Byzantium, comprise seven works located around the eastern Mediterranean rim. The original list inspired innumerable versions through the ages, often listing seven entries.

The seven ancient wonders are , The great pyramid of Giza, Hanging garden of Babylon , Temple of Artemis ,The statue of Zeus at Olympia, Colossus of Rhodes ,Light house of Alexandria ,Mausoleum of Halicarnassus. The only outstanding wonder of all is the great pyramid of Giza.

Chapter 1: The Great Pyramid Of Giza

The great pyramid of Giza is nearly 150 m tall* and 230 m wide at the base. The average block of stone used in building this pyramid has dimensions of .66 m x 1.00 m x 1.50 m.

The ancient Egyptians transported these blocks from the quarry to the pyramid on wooden sleds. These blocks were quarried at a site on the Giza Plateau that shall be taken to be about 5 km away although it may have been closer.

In order to pull the blocks to the required heights, the Egyptians built earthen ramps that greatly reduced the slope of the pyramid side, While the ground in front of the sled's skids is lubricated to make it easier to pull the blocks. The pyramid was build in twenty years , in this fashion, the Egyptians was working for the glorification of their Kings.

The Egyptians built earthen ramps that greatly reduced the slope of the pyramid side in order to pull the blocks to the required heights. The pyramid of Giza blocks were made of sandstone with a density of about 2.00 g/cm3. The Egyptian's sled system had a rather high coefficient of static friction (m= 0.7) but a much lower coefficient of kinetic friction (m= 0.3**).

The date of construction was 2584–2561 BC

The modern location to the North was Giza Mecropolis 29 degrees, 58 degrees, 45.03 degrees north.

And the modern location to the East was 31 degrees,08 degrees,03.69 degrees East. While the major builders were Egyptians.

Discretion for the great pyramid of Giza

If you would like to visit the first and the best tourist attraction of the world, then I suggested you visit the land of pharaoh and you have a live experience of what Egypt's Top tourist attraction was. These Great Pyramids of Giza since inception belongs to the existing member of the Seven Wonders of the World.

In front of the three main pyramids of Giza in Egypt which are Great Pyramid of Khufu, the Pyramid of Kafhre and the Pyramid of Menkaura., there lies the cat-like sculpture, the Sphinx, which attracts millions of tourists annually. Each pyramid is a tomb of the Kings of Egypt.

GETTING TO THIS PYRAMID

There are always trips to where these amazing pyramids were planted , so getting to them is always easy as these pyramids is always the major attraction of Egypt, however you can take a taxi from the center of Cairo, at times taxi are quite substantial but there are regular air conditioned bus as well to be preferred, all you have to do is check on the time table, it's really comfortable and I bet you will love the experience.

GETTING IN AND ARROUND THESE PYRAMIDS

First of all if you are suffering from claustrophobia, you may waive the option of going inside because it is very narrow inside

Since the 1980's it is strictly forbidden climbing up to the pyramids, is better trying preserving and not ruining a Wonder of the World, just for fun. As a matter of fact there are plenty of options for getting around the pyramids as you can walk, take a horse or take a camel ride.

EXPERIENCE THE LIGHT AND SOUND SHOW BY THE PYRAMIDS.

It is a real fun at night, there is an experience of sounds in different languages and light show around the pyramids about its history.

LET'S GET READY

First of all make sure that you have plenty of water around you, wear sunscreens, hat and avoid wearing darker cloths, do not forget that months in Egypt are very hot.

So it is advised to get prepared in other to enjoy the most of your holiday and enjoy your stay in the country of the pyramids.

October to May is always the peak travel season and the fairer season than May to October when the temperature is very high.

Also during the Ramadan, mostly the attractions are always closed , and also alcohol are not as well available as usual.

Chapter 2: The Hanging Garden Of Babylon

The Hanging from the latin world 'pensilis' and the greek word 'kremastos' Gardens of Babylon is a current member of the Seven Ancient Wonders of the World because there is really no strong evidence saying that this was even a real place.

While working on an inscription of the Assyrian king Sennacherib, who reigned a century earlier than Nebuchadnezzar, I began to realize that details of his palace and garden at Nineveh matched some of the extraordinary details of the Hanging Garden described by the later Greek writers, not least the raising of water up the garden high up on the citadel mound, by means of an Archimedean screw long before the lifetime of Archimedes himself. Sennacherib described his palace with its garden as 'a wonder for all peoples'.

But also from this wonder, the first advanced hydraulic hand pumps were formed, and it was a gift for a king.

The Hanging Gardens of Babylon were built near the Euphrates River in modern-day Iraq by the Babylonian king Nebuchadrezzar II around 600 B.C who ruled the city for 43 years according to ancient Greek poets. There is an alternative story that the gardens were built by the Assyrian Queen Semiramis during her five year reign starting in 810 BC). This was the height of the city's power and influence and King Nebuchadnezzar is known to have constructed an astonishing array of temples, streets, palaces and walls. It was on a huge square brick terrace that was laid out in steps like a theater that the gardens was planted and was as high 75 feet in the air. The tower garden was purposely built by the king to ease his lover Amytis' homesickness for the natural beauty of her home in Media , it was situated in the northwestern part of modern-day Iran. Then it was later described how people could walk underneath the beautiful gardens, which rested on tall stone columns. Modern scientists have confirmed that for the gardens to survive they would have had to be irrigated using a system consisting of a pump, waterwheel and cisterns to carry water from the Euphrates many feet into the air. As a result, most modern scholars believe that the existence of the gardens was part of an inspired and widely believed but still fictional tale.

Though there are multiple accounts of the gardens in both Greek and Roman literature, none of them are firsthand, and no mention of the gardens has been found in Babylonian cuneiform inscriptions.

The Hanging Gardens perhaps did not really "hang" in the sense of being suspended from cables or ropes. The name comes from an inexact translation of the Greek word kremastos, or the Latin word pensilis, which means that not just "hanging", but "overhanging" as in the case of a terrace or balcony.

At the top of the garden, Greek writers described a pillared walkway roofed with layers of matting and soil so that trees grew above it. A drawing made in the mid-nineteenth century, of a panel of sculpture now lost, showed just such a pillared walkway at the top of a garden. The drawing is preserved in the British Museum. The original panel was part of an Assyrian palace at Nineveh.

The Greek geographer Strabo, who described the gardens in first century BC, wrote, "It consists of vaulted terraces raised one above another, and resting upon cube-shaped pillars. These are hollow and filled with earth to allow trees of the largest size to be planted. The pillars, the vaults, and terraces are constructed of baked brick and asphalt."

About the water transfer from and to the garden - One of the solutions that the designers of the garden may have used to move the water, however, was a "chain pump. This was an immense task given as a result of the lack of modern engines and pressure pumps in the fifth century B.C..

A chain pump with two large wheels, one above the other, connected by a chain. On the chain are hung buckets. Below the lower wheel is a pool with the water source. As the wheel is turned, the buckets slips into the water pool and pick up the water. The chain then lifts them to the upper wheel, where the buckets are tipped and dumped into an upper pool. The chain then decend the empty buckets down to be refilled.

The artificial streams to water the gardens comes from pool at the top of the gardens which then be released by gates into channels. The beneath pump wheel was connected to a shaft and a handle. Also the slaves were provided to run the mechanism and turning the handle.

Some personal research confirmed that water was conducted on to the citadel via canals and aqueducts from a gorge in mountains over 90 km away. This remarkable engineering work was studied between the two World Wars, and in recent times has been enriched by tracking from early satellite photos. Alexander the Great would have admired it when he camped nearby with his army before the Battle of Gaugamela. Sennacherib had inherited from his father rule over the city of Babylon, but after his son as regent was abducted by enemies, in his fury he removed the city's gods to Assyria, so that

Nineveh, his capital city, became as if a new 'Babylon'. When the Assyrian empire came to an end, around 612 BC, Nineveh was not totally destroyed, as Hebrew prophets described with typical literary exaggeration. It continued to be inhabited, rising again to become the great city that Jonah found, and which was well known to historians of the Roman empire.

Regardless of the massive Walls of Babylon and the Ishtar Gate, the 300 foot high ziggurat, the Tower of Babel and all of the beautiful architecture and cultural displays that existed at Babylon, every traveler would have been amazed of seeing the Kings palace with all sorts of vegetation spilling out over the sides. Towering over 400 feet above the flat landscape, this would have been a structure seen from miles away.

The flora of the Hanging Gardens of Babylon was unique in that it did not contain typical flowers and small plants. Instead the Gardens were full of trees that towered high over the landscape along with all sorts of exotic plants and animals within the structure itself. These trees were most likely indigenous to the areas surrounding the Middle East and were probably collected from throughout the Empire and its vast trading networks.

THE CONSTRUCTION SCOPE OF THE HANGING GARDEN OF BABYLON.

The Construction of the garden was majorly by having to avoid having the liquid ruining the foundations once it was released it wasn't only intricated by getting the water up to the top,

Babel achitecture make use of bricks mostly, Since stone was difficult to get on the Mesopotamian plain. The bricks comprises clay mixed with chopped straw and baked in the sun with bitumen .The bricks quickly dissolved when soaked with water woefully, because of the substance which they were made, However, the gardens were continually exposed to irrigation and the underneath had to be protected, For most buildings in Babel this wasn't a problem because rain was too scarce.

Another research confirmed that Eight years after conquering Babylon, ruler Sennacherib began to experience a series of revolts within the city led by Mushezib-Marduk. When it got too violent he had Babylon destroyed and razed to the ground in 689 BCE. He then scattered the ruins around all over the desert. It is highly unlikely that any Gardens would have existed at Babylon at this time as Old Babylon was completely destroyed. So either they were truly indeed the Hanging Gardens of Nineveh or they existed during a later time period that formed the original theory.

In his razing and utter decimation of Babylon, Sennacherib spelled out his own fate as he was assassinated by his own sons with support from the High Court. His destruction of Babylon was viewed as pretty serious offense within the religious culture of Mesopotamia. He was succeeded in power by his youngest son Esarhaddon who rebuilt Babylon to its former glory under his rule. It was during this time that Babylon became known as a center for learning and culture. Esarhaddon was quick to rebuild relations with Babylon and spent half of the year there along with improving the city.

The ten Major facts about the hanging garden of Babylon

The location - The city state of Babylon was in the Modern Iraq

Building time - It was actually built around 600 BC

Its function - was basically a royal garden of the king Nebuchadnezzar to please him and his wife Amytis.

The gardens destruction - The destruction of the garden was caused by the earthquake, second century BC.

Some historians argue that the mud-brick construction of the time would not have left physical evidence after the destruction of the wonder, while others suggest the true site may have become obscured when the rivers of Babylon changed their course. One possible explanation for this discrepancy is that the legend of the Hanging Gardens became intertwined with an actual construction elsewhere in the region. Archaeologists discovered the remnants of an extensive terraced garden near the ancient city of Nineveh in the Assyrian Empire, possibly built by

Sennacherib much earlier than Nebuchadnezzar's reign. After conquering Babylon in 689 B.C., Sennacherib often referred to Nineveh as "the new Babylon," possibly contributing to the confusion.

The size of the garden - The garden's height was approximately 80ft, and that's about 24m, 56miles longer

Fortresses and temples in the gardens contain immense statues of solid gold.

King Nebuchadnezzar ruled the city of Babylon for 43 years.

The pillars, vaults and terraces were built with baked brick and asphalt.

What is it made of - It's made of mud brick waterproofed with lead.

The Hanging Gardens of Babylon had plants cultivated above ground level, and the roots of the trees are embedded in an upper terrace rather than the earth.

In the 'Hanging Gardens', the plants did not actually hang. They grew from many different levels of terraces (similar to balconies).

Other things to know - Sincerely some archeologists suggest that the actual location was 350 miles to the north in the city of Nineveh or Hillah 37°56'59"N and 44.4275°E and not in Babylon.

Here's the map to the Babylonian empire

Here are some of the major contributions of the Babylonian Empire to civilization which include building the Hanging Gardens of Babylon, considered as one of the ancient seven world wonders; fashioning jewelry; using contracts for commercial transactions; developing two significant literary pieces; and establishing the Code of Hammurabi, which became the foundation for many existing laws in modern times. Babylon, serving as the capital of the empire, was a powerful city-state in the ancient region of Mesopotamia.

Also The Babylonian Empire was one of two new empires that emerged and gained prominence after the downfall of the Akkadian Empire. The Semitic Amorites of Babylon were known to have originated the craft of jewelry-making by using precious stones and metals. At the heart of their economy was forming sales contracts and validating their business dealings with seals. The Babylonians are also noted for producing the epics of Gilgamesh and Enuma Elish, two of the oldest literary works that are still being studied today.

Perhaps the most famous among the Amorites was Hammurabi. He wielded his power with intelligence and a firm hand. Within a short period of ascending the throne, he successfully united the vast majority of the Mesopotamian territories. Hammurabi is chiefly renowned for compiling the first written set of laws, known as the Code of Hammurabi, which encompassed the various aspects of life during that time.

The termination of Babylon –

After Alexander the Great's death his generals fought over who would gain control over the empire in the Wars of the Diadochi. Alexander the Great infamously said before he died it should go to the strongest, and they all each assumed it was them. A war broke out and Babylon was right in the center of it. Facing constant internal strife for years the city slowly deteriorated over time as the residents fled for safer places. Babylon was eventually controlled by Seleucus I who established the Seleucid Empire in the region of eastern Asia. According to a tablet discovered the population of Babylon was transported to the new Hellenistic capital city of Seleucia in 275 BC, which would have meant the final end for the city of Babylon. Without the workforce and man power necessary to operate something as intense as the gardens the structure could not have continued to exist and most likely fell into ruin along with the rest of the city. As the people abandoned the canals necessary to sustain life in the region the entire area gradually turned back into desert and the ruins of their city buried underneath the sands.

Chapter 3: The Temple Of Artemis

A Sion Antipater said, i have set eyes on the wall of lofty Babylon on which is a road for chariots, and the huge labour of the high pyramids and the statue of Zeus by the Alpheus, and the vast tomb of Mausolus and the Colossus of the Sun, and the hanging gardens but when I saw the house of Artemis that mounted to the clouds, those other marvels lost their brilliancy, and I said, 'Lo, apart from Olympus, the Sun never looked on aught so grand.

Standing in a field near Selcuk Turkey is one lone column surrounded by scattered ancient remains of a once great ancient Greek structure. Here once stood the magnificent Temple of Artemis at Ephesus one of the Seven Wonders of the Ancient World. The most majestic accomplishment of Greek civilization and Hellenistic culture, built as a tribute to Artemis – the Greek goddess of the hunt, mistress of Nature, protector of wild beasts and the sister of Apollo is The greatest temple of the ancient world called the Temple of Artemis .

In the modern day Turkey, this magnificent temple was situated in Ephesus which has a plan to become the best seaport in Asia minor was regarded as one of the seven wonders of the ancient world.

It minorly consists of one hundred and twenty seven iconic marble column each standing 60ft (20 metres). is one lone column surrounded by scattered ancient remains of a once great ancient Greek structure. Here once stood the magnificent Temple of Artemis at Ephesus one of the Seven Wonders of the Ancient World.The temple was first built in 6th century BC as a replacement for older temples, the building was so spectacular that one ancient writer, who claims to have seen all the seven wonders at first hand, was more impressed with it even than he was of the pyramids of Egypt! It reached, he said, into the clouds and then later destroyed 200years later by wide fire and then rebuilt under the supervision of the great Alexandra.

When the Greeks colonised the eastern Aegean, long before the building of this famous Temple, there was a temple already on the site at

Ephesus; there had been since the Bronze Age. The goddess worshipped there was almost certainly a form of Cybele, and when the Greeks arrived she was incorporated into the Greek pantheon as Artemis, goddess of the woodland and of the moon, and sister to Apollo, the sun.

From an engraving of a Greek replica of the famous image of Artemis at the Temple at Ephesus, and a surviving statue of Artemis of the 1st century AD, it is clear that she had a large number of decorative features that have been variously interpreted as breasts or eggs, hanging about her chest...'

'Well, eggs or breasts or fruit, she was certainly a fertility goddess,' said Miranda, 'But we will never know for sure what her statue looked like, because by the end of the fourth century the local Christians had used what remained of the temple as a stone quarry.

In 268 AD, the great temple of Artemis actually got destroyed by an invasion of earthquake, robbers (plunderes) and gothic hordes, an East Germanic tribe.

But today , the once glorious structure remains only the solitary colums of it.

The great Temple of Artemis became celebrated and continues to inspire as one of the notable products of the competence ,mastery and innovation of early civilizations of the earth, also recognized as the Artemesium or Artemision. During the ancient times the Temple of Artemis has also made a remarkable and historical benefaction to many people. The temple became an important attraction, visited by merchants, kings, and sightseers, many of whom paid homage to Artemis in the form of jewelry and various goods. It also offered sanctuary to those fleeing persecution or punishment, a tradition linked in myth to the Amazons who twice fled there seeking the goddess' protection from punishment, firstly by Dionysus and later, by Heracles. Since then and until now, this place is one of the favorites for visitors to take a glimpse. We all know how memorable and significant it symbolize in the lives of ancient people. The temple's design was not of the common rectangle portico, but a combination of Near-Eastern design and Classic Greek and execution. According to the research, the marble constructed in the temple made it unique among all other temple around the world. The primitive wonder or Artemis has diverse works of art by most brilliant artists including bronze statues of the Amazons.

The Temple of Artemis has the statue of Artemis goddess which was placed in the center of the temple and probably made around 800 BC on a swampy strip discovered at the bank of river in Ephesus. This statue was the major component of it which is worshiped by Greek people.

The Statue first got placed in the Temple of Artemis but the statue of Diana was taken by British people and it's now laced in a museum of United Kingdom where many other ornaments of this temple kept there, after the fall down of the temple.

Few interesting fact to know about the temple of Artemis -

Since inception, the Artemis Temple might have ever been the first temple to be built of marble.

Additionally, it can also be the first building history ever constructed made of marble.

Artemis was considered as the goddess of the hunt and goddess of the moon, she was as well the daughter of Leto and Zeus, and an Olympian God . She is as well confirmed as Apollo's twin sister.

The built of the second temple was around four times bigger in compass than the first one.

The Temple of Artemis is also acknowledged as the Temple of Diana.

The Artemis temple was on indistinguishable site every time it was rebuilt.

The temple was severally utilized as a worship house and as a marketplace.

Before its final destruction this amazing example of Greek Architecture had 121 columns each standing 60 feet high (18.3 meters). Sadly only one remains; the others were torn down centuries ago for use in other ancient construction projects. Several of the columns are believed to have been used in the construction of a former Greek Orthodox Church named Hagia Sophia in Istanbul Turkey built between 537 AD and 1453 AD.

The temple stood in the ancient city of Ephesus which was part of ancient Greece. This site is now within Turkey near modern day Selcuk.

The Antipater of Sidon, who created the list of Seven Wonders of the World, defined Artemis as being more awe-inspiring than other six wonders and stated that although each one of these sites was very beautiful they were not even close to the splendor of the Temple of Artemis. The temple was mentioned in the Christian Bible in Acts 19:35, where the temple is called the Temple of Diana. The temple was influenced by many different religions from faraway lands; and the priests and high priests from each one of these religions came to Ephesus to worship. It wasn't until the year 1869, after a 60 year search, that an expedition from the British Museum found fragments of the statues and other artifacts. Today, the only remnant from the temple lies near Selcuk, Turkey. No one knows why the temple has never been rebuilt; or what happened to the believers. For this reason you can understand why the Temple of Artemis is considered to be one of the greatest unsolved mysteries of ancient history.

Artemis temple is such a great place to visit with your family and friends. It will serve as your adventurous travel while on vacation and your money and time is worth the cost.

The Ephesian Artemis was unique though Artemis' shrines, temples and festivals (Artemisia) could be found throughout the Greek world.

The Ephesians considered her theirs, and resented any foreign claims to her protection. Once Persia ousted and replaced their Lydian overlord Croesus, the Ephesians played down his contribution to the Temple's restoration. On the whole, the Persians dealt fairly with Ephesus, but removed some religious artifacts from Artemis' Temple to Sardis and brought Persian priests into her Ephesian cult; this was not forgiven. When Alexander conquered the Persians, his offer to finance the Temple's second rebuilding was politely but firmly refused. Ephesian Artemis lent her city's diplomacy a powerful religious edge

Like the Artemis temple has demonstrated, there are no other temples that can make a historic and notable works of architecture and arts.

Discovering the temple today

It was then in 1869 that the site was rediscovered by an expedition led by john wood that was sponsored by the British museum. These excavation continues until 1874, some fragment of sculpture were found during the 1904 – 1906 excavation directed by David Hogarth.

The recovered sculptured fragments of the 4th-century reconstructing and a few from the earlier temple, which had been used in the wreckage fill for the rebuilding, were assembled and laced in the "Ephesus Room" of the British Museum. Again in the 7th century BC, a flood destroyed the temple, depositing over half a meter of sand and flotsam over the original clay floor In addition, the museum has part of possibly the oldest pot-hoard of coins in the world (600 BC) that had been buried in the foundations of the Archaic temple.

Today the site of the temple was located near the ancient city of Ephesus, about 75 km south from the modern port city of İzmir, in Turkey. Today which lies just near Selçuk, is known by a single column constructed of detached fragments discovered on the site. And the bearing of the modern location is just 37°56′59″N and 27°21′50″E.

Chapter 4: The Statue Of Zeus At Olympia

The statue of Zeus was erected nearly 2,500 years ago in Olympia, Greece. Once built as a shrine to honor the Greek god Zeus, this statue was regarded the incarnate of the Greeks' most salient and dominant god, and not to have seen it at least once in one's lifetime was considered a misfortune. The statue of zeus was actually one of the seven wonders of the ancient world and arguably the most famous statue of it's day.

This is the statue of the god in whose honor the Ancient Olympic games were held. It was located on the land that gave its very name to the Olympics.

The Statue of Zeus would have been an astonishing and awesome sight as it towered over the ancient city of Olympia instilling fear and devotion to the god of the Greeks.

The colossal statue was created by Greek sculptor Phidias and stood 43 feet tall , it was so tall that its head nearly touched the top of the temple. It was an astounding achievement during that time. By the standards of the day. The statue is said to have been erected in the Temple of Zeus. This statue was the representation of God Zeus who was depicted as sitting on a beautiful cedar wood throne that was adornment ornamented with gold, ivory, precious stones and ebony, aswell

The statue depicted the god of thunder seated bare-chested at a wooden throne.

It was stated that this richly crafted statue requires lot of care as the place where it was stationed was quite damp and there was a probability of getting destroyed due to humidity, therefore Olive oil was constantly applied on the statue which helped to keep the wood in undestroyed. a research source suggests that the chair has wonderful carvings of animals and Greek Gods carved well in the chair. In the right hand of Greek God Zeus, there was a figurine. There was an eagle perched on left hand of Zeus.

About its symbol of power - The ability to construct such an impressive powerful statue have made the Greek people proud of their country and made visitors envious. A dual strategy of military power and impressive civilization was employed by the Greeks and later the Romans to build impressive empires. Besides stimulating the Greeks to fear and love their serving god's, the Zeus status also served another important purpose. For the Greek people and visitors alike, the statue demonstrated the power and wealth of the Greek empire. An ancient text, written by Greek geographer Pausanias, gave an account of the site where the statue was constructed.

About its destruction - In the year 1970 a massive earthquake caused major damage to the status but it was repaired soon and most of it was restored.

Archaeologists used this information to pin point the exact location where they found terracotta molds of the statue and personal items which carried the sculptor's name. According to legend, the sculptor Phidias asked Zeus for a sign of his approval after finishing the statue; soon after, the temple was struck by lightning. The Zeus statue graced the temple at Olympia for more than eight centuries before Christian priests persuaded the Roman emperor to close the temple in the fourth century A.D. At that time, the statue was moved to a temple in Constantinople, where it is believed to have been destroyed in a fire in the year 462. Although the exact time and reason for the loss of the Statue of Zeus is not so clear as there are evidences to suggest that Roman Emperor Caligula ordered the statue to be dismantled and moved to Rome. There have been written accounts that this was not carried out before Caligula's assassination. Roman historian Suetonius wrote that the scaffold fell and the workers ran from the site in fear of Zeus.

Few facts about the statue of zeus –

The reason why the statue was built is to honor Zeus, who was the Greek Good. which is why this statue was laced in the Olympia temple. The Olympic Games were held to honor Zeus who was regarded as the 'Father of gods and men'. The games were held once in every four years and brought several thousands of sports enthusiasts in the region.

The building time duration of the statue – It took the sculptor 12 years to complete this masterpiece. It was built from the years 430-422 BC, while the construction of the statue is 435BC.

The ancient Greek calendar starts in 776 BC, for the Olympic games are believed to have started that year. The magnificent temple of Zeus was designed by the architect Libon and was finished around 450 BC. Under the growing power of ancient Greece, the simple Doric-style temple seemed too mundane, and modifications were needed. The solution: A majestic statue. The Athenian sculptor Pheidias was assigned for the "sacred" task, reminiscent of Michelangelo's paintings at the Sistine Chapel.

For the years that followed, the temple attracted visitors and worshippers from all over the world. In the second century BC repairs were skillfully made to the aging statue. In the first century AD, the Roman emperor Caligula attempted to transport the statue to Rome. However, his attempt failed when the scaffolding built by Caligula's workmen collapsed. After the Olympic games were banned in AD 391 by the emperor

Theodosius I as Pagan practices, the temple of Zeus was ordered closed.

Few descriptions –

Pheidias began working on the statue around 440 BC. Years earlier, he had developed a technique to build enormous gold and ivory statues. This was done by erecting a wooden frame on which sheets of metal and ivory were placed to provide the outer covering. Pheidias' workshop in Olympia still exists, and is coincidentally -- or may be not -- identical in size and orientation to the temple of Zeus. There, he sculpted and carved the different pieces of the statue before they were assembled in the temple.

When the statue was completed, it barely fitted in the temple. Strabo wrote.

although the temple itself is very large, the sculptor is criticized for not having appreciated the correct proportions. He has shown Zeus seated, but with the head almost touching the ceiling, so that we have the impression that if Zeus moved to stand up he would unroof the temple.

Strabo was right, except that the sculptor is to be commended, not criticized. It is this size impression that made the statue so wonderful. It is the idea that the king of gods is capable of unroofing the temple if he stood up that fascinated poets and historians alike. The base of the statue was about 6.5 m (20 ft) wide and 1.0 meter (3 ft) high. The height of the statue itself was 13 m (40 ft), equivalent to a modern 4-story building.

The statue was so high that visitors described the throne more than Zeus body and features. The legs of the throne were decorated with sphinxes and winged figures of Victory. Greek gods and mythical figures also adorned the scene: Apollo, Artemis, and Niobe's children. The Greek Pausanias wrote

The statue was occasionally decorated with gifts from kings and rulers. the most notable of these gifts was a woollen curtain "adorned with Assyrian woven patterns and Pheonician dye" which was dedicated by the Syrian king Antiochus IV.

Copies of the statue were made, including a large prototype at Cyrene (Libya). None of them, however, survived to the present day. Early reconstructions such as the one by von Erlach are now believed to be rather inaccurate. For us, we can only wonder about the true appearance of the statue -- the greatest work in Greek sculpture.

The major builders were the Greeks .The destruction was between 5th -6th centuries AD.

The modern location was Olympia, Greece 37°38'16.3"N 21°37'48"E.

At the ancient town of Olympia, on the west coast of modern Greece, about 150 km west of Athens.

Chapter 5: Colossus Of Rhodes

The city was the target of a Macedonian blockade early in the fourth century B.C. and, according to legend, the Rhodianssold the tools and equipment left behind by the Macedonians to pay for the Colossus. The Colossus was an huge bronze sculpture of the sun god Helios, posed nude, with a spear in one hand and a torch held high in the other, built by the Rhodian sculptor chares of Lindos who has been involved with large scale statues before.

Factual source published in an article in 2008 by Ursula Vedder suggests that the Colossus was never in the port, but rather was part of the Acropolis of Rhodes, on a hill today named Monte Smith, which overlooks the port area. The temple on top of Monte Smith is traditionally thought to have been devoted to Apollo, but according to Vedder, it would have been a Helios sanctuary. The huge stone foundations at the temple site, the function of which is not definitively known by modern scholars, are proposed by Vedder to have been the supporting platform of the Colossus. Another Media reports in 1989 initially suggested that huge stones found on the seabed off the coast of Rhodes might have been the remains of the Colossus, but this theory was later shown to be without merit.

The construction of the statue lasted over twelveyears in the third century B.C. It was stated that 13.6 tons of bronze and 8.2 tons of iron were used in the construction therefore there was a shortage of bronze in the ancient world during colossus's construction.

The colossus was designed by the sculptor Chares, the statue was, at 100 feet, the tallest of the ancient world.

Although it was originally believed and is often portray as Helios standing with one foot on each side of the harbor, but most scholars now agree that the statue's legs were most likely built close together to support its immense weight aswell research agree the statue's colossal form could not have supported its weight in a straddled position. Although descriptions of the statue differ slightly, most agree the Colossus of Rhodes was made upon a frame of iron bars with brass or bronze sheets attached to the bars to represent the skin. It was completed around 280 B.C. The Colossus of Rhodes stood regally near the entrance to the harbor and stood for sixty years until it was tumbled in an earthquake and was never rebuilt and The Remains of the colossus were on its site around 800 years and they impressed to the travelers that saw them. Even there was an offer by the Egyptian King, Ptolemy, to pay for the statue to be rebuilt, was refused by the Rhodians, who believed that the god Helios had used the earthquake to demolish the statue because it offended him in some way. Even the remain ruins of the colossus were laid downon the ground for years. Story research verifies that the fingers of the Colossus were bigger than most known statues. An Arab force under Muslim caliph Muawiyah I captured Rhodes in 653, and according to The Chronicle of Theophanes the Confessor, the statue was cast down and sold to a Jewish merchant of Edessa who loaded the bronze on 900 camels. The Arab destruction and the purported sale to a Jew possibly originated as a powerful metaphor for Nebuchadnezzar's dream of the destruction of a great statue. Another research confirmed that the ruins were pieces by conquering Arabs in the seventh century, carted away by 900 camels, and was sold out as metal scraps. An alternative by engineers of today states the feet would have been carved of stone and enveloped with bronze plates riveted in place.

The same story is recorded by Bar Hebraeus, writing in Syriac in the 13th century in Edessa, (after the Arab pillage of Rhodes) "And a great number of men hauled on strong ropes which were tied round the brass Colossus which was in the city and pulled it down. And they weighed from it three thousand loads of Corinthian brass, and they sold it to a certain Jew from Emesa" (the Syrian city of Homs). Theophanes is the sole source of this account and all other sources can be traced to him.

The base pedestal was at least 60 feet (18 m) in diameter and either circular or octagonal. The feet were carved in stone and covered with thin bronze plates riveted together. Eight forged iron bars set in a radiating horizontal position formed the ankles and turned up to follow the lines of the legs while becoming progressively smaller. Individually cast curved bronze plates 60 inches (1,500 mm) square with turned-in edges were joined together by rivets through holes formed during casting to form a series of rings. The lower plates were 1 inch (25 mm) in thickness to the knee and 3/4 inch thick from knee to abdomen, while the upper plates were 1/4 to 1/2 inch thick.

Bronze plates covering the iron frame would have been 1-inch thick to the knee and progressively thinner moving up the body. Additional stabilization would have been needed at the neck, shoulder, and other joints. The legs of the statue would have needed to be packed to the knees with rocks to stabilize the immense height of the statue.

In the recent times, group of European scientists, architects, and engineers have proposed a new, even taller version of the statue to be built in Greece, serving as a museum, library, and cultural center. The statue will also hold a light beacon that can be seen for 34 miles away directly over its head, and be covered in/exclusively powered by solar panels—both elements quite appropriate for the God of the Sun

The modern location is Rhodes, Greece 36°27'04"N 28°13'40"E

Chapter 6: Light House Of Alexandria

The light house of Alexandria was designed by the Greek architect Sostratos, while the major builders are Greeks, Ptolemaic Egyptians . The Construction of the light house of Alexandria began on the 280 BCE, After Alexander the Great died of a fever at age 32, and commissioned its construction shortly thereafter.Originallycommissioned by Ptolemy I, but the project was finished by his son. Ptolemy II Philadelphus.

During the reign of Ptolemy II, the lighthouse helped to guide Nile River ships in and out of the city's busy harbor. It took twelve years to complete, at a total cost of 800 talents, and served as a prototype for all later lighthouses in the world.

On which the lighthouse was depicted, the Archeologists have found ancient coins, and from them deduced that the structure had three tiers, a square level at the bottom, an octagonal level in the middle and a cylindrical top. A large curved mirror or polished disc at the top of the lighthouse was used to project the light from a fire in front of the disc.

Above the cylindrical top , that stood a 16-foot statue, most likely of Ptolemy II or Alexander the Great, that was whom the city was named. Although estimates of the lighthouse's height have ranged from 200 to 600 feet, most modern scholars believe it was about 380 feet tall.

The light was produced by a furnace at the top, and the tower was said to have been built mostly with solid blocks of limestone.

Research reported that Sostratus had a dedication inscribed in metal letters to the "Saviour Gods". Later Pliny the Elder wrote that Sostratus was the architect, which is disputed. In the second century AD the satirist Lucian wrote that Sostratus inscribed his name under plaster bearing the name of Ptolemy. Today's city development lying between the present Grand Square and the modern Ras al-Tiin quarter is built on the silt which gradually widened and obliterated this mole, and Ras al-Tiin represents all that is left of the island of Pharos, the site of the lighthouse at its eastern point having been weathered away by the sea.

The other category of findings consists of much heavier blocks of granite – 49 to 69 tons. The fact that some were broken into two or three pieces indicates that they fell from a great height. Empereur's team is convinced that these are remnants of the lighthouse. Several dozen pieces have already been raised, restored and are currently on view in the open-air amphitheatre of Kom el Dikka, in Alexandria.

The discoveries opened new perspectives for Egyptian archaeologists. Just few months ago, the CSA created a department of underwater archaeology.

The lighthouse gradually fell into disrepair and was persistently damaged by Crete earthquakes from 956 to 1323.

Whatever ruins remained on the site were removed or reused for the building of a medieval fort, constructed on the same location in 1480.

Under the discovery of the ruins – Strange figures were noticed under the waters around Pharos, off the coast of Alexandria, Egypt. Dive down six or eight meters and you'll find yourself face to face with sphinxes and colossal statues of men and women. A stone torso of a woman from the third-century B.C. Pharos of Alexandria - a lighthouse that was one of the seven wonders of the ancient world - has been salvaged from the Mediterranean Sea. A number of sculptures in the sea around a fifteenth-century fortress built by the Mamluke sultan Qait Bay had been reported in a 1974 article in Nautical Archaeology, which suggested that the Pharos might have stood on the site. In 1993, when the Egyptian government began building a concrete breakwater around the base of the fortress to protect it from storm damage, there was an outcry from archaeologists who feared the operation might destroy any surviving remains of the Pharos and other nearby ancient buildings. The project was temporarily halted, and scholars from the Egyptian Supreme Council of Antiquities and the French Centre d'Études Alexandrines, led by Jean-Yves Empereur, began searching the waters around the fortress. According to Chris Scarre of Cambridge University, "Their finds confirm that one side of the Pharos collapsed into the sea, and that much material from this amazing structure still lies scattered on the seabed. Only now can we begin to appreciate the true extent and importance of the remains." In addition to the torso, Empereur's team has recovered some 30 other sculptures not from the Pharos, including sphinxes, granite columns and capitals, a fragment of an obelisk with a hieroglyphic inscription, and a headless statue of the pharaoh Ramesses II (ca. 1290-1224 B.C.). How and when the construction of the breakwater will resume has not yet been settled .As a result ,the remains of the lighthouse have been discovered in the water and today, especially some of its remains have since been discovered at the bottom of the Nile, so it is possible to see the pieces while scuba diving.

The modern location is in Alexandria, Egypt 31°12'50"N 29°53'08"E.

Chapter 7: Mausoleum At Halicarnassus

Mausoleum at Halicarnassus or Tomb of Mausolus was a tomb built between 353 and 350 BC at Halicarnassus, presently located in Bodrum, Turkey for Mausolus, a satrap in the Persian Empire, and his sister-wife Artemisia II of Caria.

The structure was designed by the Greek architects Satyros and Pythius of Priene. In another way , Mausolus was also Artemisia's brother, and, according to research, she was so grief-stricken at his passing that she mixed his ashes with water and drank them in addition to ordering the mausoleum's construction.

The mausoleum was rectangular in structure, with base dimensions of about 40 m by 30 m and The finished structure of the mausoleum was considered to be such an aesthetic triumph that Antipater of Sidon identified it as one of his Seven Wonders of the Ancient World The podium that overlied the edifice was adorned with statues. The burial chamber and the sacrophagus were made of white alabaster decorated with gold.

They were situated on the podium and surrounded by Ionic columns. There was a pyramid roof decorated with myriad statues, which was supported by a colonnade.

The tomb top was adorned with the statue of a chariot pulled by four horses.

The beauty of the mausoleum lay not in its grand structure but in the life size and often larger than life size statues of people, lions, horses, and other animals in varying scale.

The word "mausoleum" came about because of this tomb for King Mausolus—"mausoleum" now officially refers to a building above ground that serves as a burial chamber and monument.

The massive mausoleum was about 148 feet high and entirely made of white marble .The building's complex design, consisting of three rectangular layers, may have been an attempt to reconcile Lycian, Greek and Egyptian architectural styles.

The first layer was a 60-foot base of steps, followed by a middle layer of 36 Ionic columns and a stepped, pyramid-shaped roof. At the very top of the roof lay the tomb, decorated by the work of four sculptors, and a 20-foot marble rendition of a four-horse chariot. The mausoleum was successively destroyed in the earthquake from 12th to 15th century and its remains were later used in the fortification of a castle. In 1846, pieces of one of the mausoleum's friezes were extracted from the castle and now reside, along with other relics from the Halicarnassus site, in London's British Museum and the Knights of John of Malta, used few stone blocks in this structure to construct a castle. Another source confirmed that Suleiman the Magnificent conquered the base of the knights on the island of Rhodes, who then relocated first briefly to Sicily and later permanently to Malta, leaving the Castle and Bodrum to the Ottoman Empire. Artemisia lived for only two years after the death of her husband. The burns with their ashes were placed in the yet unfinished tomb. As a form of sacrifice ritual the bodies of a large number of dead animals were placed on the stairs leading to the tomb, and then the stairs were filled with stones and rubble, sealing the access. According to the historian Pliny the Elder, the craftsmen decided to stay and finish the work after the death of their patron "considering that it was at once a memorial of his own fame and of the sculptor's art.

That was how one of the seven wonders of the ancient world came to an end.

The mausoleum is unique in ancient Greek history because it only features art and statues that depict real people and animals—most other important buildings and temples featured art about mythology and the gods.

The city of Halicarnassus is now named Bodrum. Bodrum is now a major vacation destination.

It's most popular attraction, though, is not the Mausoleum at Halicarnassus ruins but rather the crusader castle that is partially made from the tomb ruins.

Sincerely if you want to consider a nice and historical place for your vacation, trust me you won't regret visiting the Mausoleum at Halicarnassus.

The modern location of Mausoleum of Halicarnassus was Bodrum, Turkey 37.0379°N 27.4241°E.

Here's the broken down of Mausoleum of Mausolus at Halicarnassus, Bodrum, Turkey.

Chapter 8: Compiling A List Of Wonders

So who, in ancient times, selected the Seven Wonders of the World? And if so many are now largely lost, how do we know so much about their appearance, how they were built – and how their fortunes fared down the centuries?

In the fourth century BC within little more than 15 years Alexander the Great expanded the Greek Empire to such an astonishing extent that it stretched from the Eastern Mediterranean all the way to India. This not only disseminated Greek culture across three continents but also allowed Greek travellers access to hitherto inaccessible parts of the ancient world and their indigenous civilisations. Essentially, these Greek travellers became like modern-day tourists, and several recorded their awestruck experiences, their writings becoming crucial sources for latter-day knowledge of the Seven Wonders.

Several lists of Wonders were compiled, but the best known is by Antipater of Sidon, a Greek writer and poet of the second century BC. His 'list' of Wonders survives in the form of a poem written c.140 BC in which he singles out the Temple of Artemis at Ephesus as the greatest Wonder of all:

"I have set eyes on the wall of lofty Babylon along which chariots race, and the statue of Zeus by the Alpheus, and the hanging gardens, and the Colossus of Helios, and the huge labour of the high pyramids, and the vast tomb of Mausolus, but when I saw the house of Artemis that mounted to the clouds, those other marvels lost their brilliancy, and I said: 'Behold, apart from Olympus, the Sun never looked on anything so grand'."

Antipater of Sidon omits the Lighthouse of Alexandria, but all seven Wonders were listed by Philo of Byzantium (c.280-220 BC), a Greek engineer and writer who probably lived most of his life in Alexandria, and whose list of Wonders became a composite with that of Antipater of Sidon to form the Seven Wonders (other lists included the Ishtar Gate at Babylon).

Other ancient writers, philosophers and historians, such as Strabo, Diodorus Siculus, Callimachus of Cyrene, Berossus and the 'father of history', Herodotus, have left us their own lists and detailed (if often second-hand) accounts, from which we have fashioned our modern-day perceptions of the Seven Wonders of the World. Many centuries later artists, architects and scholars such as Maaerten van Heemskerck (1498-1574), Pirro Ligorio (c.1510-83) and Johann Fischer von Erlach (1656-1723) used such ancient texts as the basis from which they fashioned their own fantastical images of the Seven Wonders – images that were often produced as prints and widely disseminated, thus conveying the magic of the Wonders to a much greater audience.

THE GREAT PYRAMID OF GIZA

Despite their familiarity as classic images of Egypt, the ancient civilisation's pyramids still cast their awesome spell on the modern-day visitor. (Pliny the Elder, the first-century historian, was less impressed, considering them an "idle and foolish exhibition of royal wealth".)

A text of the time describes the pyramids as being a stairway to heaven for the pharaoh's soul, and the most magnificent is undoubtedly the Great Pyramid at Giza – the culmination of centuries of pyramid construction. It also has the double distinction of being the oldest of the Seven Wonders and the only one surviving relatively intact.

And they are astounding structures. The precision and technological ingenuity involved in their construction stands as testament to the mathematical and astronomical skill of the Ancient Egyptians. They're also astonishing feats of geometrical accuracy, to such an extent that they have spawned a whole raft of theories attributing their construction to extraterrestrial forces.

A short history of pyramids

The pyramids were built as tombs for the early pharaohs and their queens of the Old Kingdom (c.2686-2181 BC) and the Middle Kingdom (c.2040-1782 BC) of Egypt, and about 80 of varying shapes and sizes survive. They evolved from the rectangular mastaba tombs of the kings of the Early Dynastic period (c.3050-2686 BC). Pyramid building began with the Third Dynasty pharaoh Djoser, who worked with his chief architect Imhotep on such constructions as his famous 'Step Pyramid' at the Saqqara necropolis near Memphis. It continued and developed under the reigns of the great pyramid builders Sneferu and his son Khufu (dubbed 'Cheops' by the Ancient Greeks).

The pyramids at Giza were built during the Old Kingdom, which saw notable advances in art, architecture and technology. This cultural flowering was driven by Egypt's increasing agricultural prosperity, itself a product of the richly fertile land that lay to either side of Egypt's eternal lifeline, the River Nile. During this time, daring advances in building technology and the vaulting ambitions of various pharaohs combined to produce such spectacular creations as the Great Pyramid at Giza and its equally monumental and enigmatic neighbour, The Great Sphinx.

The Great Sphinx, left, was built around the same time as the Great Pyramid of Giza, right.

Building a Wonder of the World

The pyramids of the Giza necropolis, just outside Cairo, are the most famous of all, their soaring height and distinctive geometry dominating their desert setting. They were built by the pharaohs Khufu, Khafra and Menkaure between about 2613 BC and 2494 BC and are part of elaborate funerary complexes.

The tallest, the Great Pyramid, built by Khufu some 4,500 years ago, soars to 480 feet, its mass calculated to be about 2.5 million cubic metres. Its architect was possibly Khufu's vizier, Hemon (or Hemiunu). While other pyramids have cores of rubble or mud bricks, the core of the Giza pyramid is of solid limestone, the vast blocks fitted together with astonishing closeness and accuracy, the whole structure perfectly aligned with the points of the compass.

In its pristine state the pyramid was covered in a gleaming case of polished white limestone, little of which remains today, and topped with a gilded capstone that glinted in the sun. An earthquake in AD 1300 loosened many of the casing stones, which were carried off to be recycled in building projects elsewhere. Flinders Petrie, the pioneering archaeologist and Egyptologist, who was the first to measure the pyramids systematically, noted that the cutting of the casing stones was so accurate that "to place such stones in exact contact would be careful work; to do so with cement in the joints almost impossible."

Fit for a pharaoh

But it's not just the external magnificence of the Great Pyramid that stuns the visitor: inside passages ascend or descend to three great burial chambers.

The first such chamber, which was never finished, was cut down into the bedrock beneath the pyramid site. Another passage ascends to a second burial chamber, known as the Queen's Chamber, which led up into the lower reaches of the pyramid and likewise remained unfinished.

Right at the heart of the Great Pyramid lies the Grand Gallery, which leads up to the King's Chamber, a construction so complex it has bred multiple theories as to its purpose beyond a mere resting place for a pharaoh. The tapering Grand

Gallery is 28 feet high, 153 feet long and about seven feet at its widest point, the King's Chamber 34 feet by 17 feet and nearly 20 feet high. The Chamber's sole content is a battered sarcophagus (as with so many of the tombs of Ancient Egypt, the Great Pyramid has fallen prey over the centuries to looting). It's also peppered with strange shafts, aligned with major stars, which may be associated with some ritual by which the pharaoh's spirit could ascend to heaven.

Despite the common assumption that the pyramids were built by armies of slaves – and some of those built by Sneferu were probably constructed by prisoners of war – it's now thought that they were built by skilled workers backed up by a vast army of paid labourers who set up their own villages in the vicinity. The Great Pyramid, for example, was probably constructed over a period of 20 years by a workforce of about 20,000.

Pyramidal buildings continued to feature in Ancient Egyptian architecture over many centuries, if on a smaller scale: during the New Kingdom (c.1570-1070 BC) the funerary chapels of private individuals still had pyramids above them. Modern tributes to the monumentality and exquisite simplicity of the pyramid include I. M. Pei's glass pyramid in the courtyard of the Louvre in Paris.

Sneferu: the pharaoh who laid the foundations

Sneferu (or Snefru as he is sometimes known) reigned c.2613-2589 BC. He made significant advances in the culture of Ancient Egypt – his name can be interpreted as 'to make beautiful'. He was one of the great pyramid builders of the Old Kingdom, an innovator who advanced pyramid-building technology and developed the concept of the pyramid as a royal resting place, paving the way for the achievements of his son and successor, Khufu (Cheops), builder of the Great Pyramid at Giza.

Three pyramids are ascribed to him: the distinctive Bent Pyramid at Dashur, with its peculiar shape and daring change in inclination in its upper reaches, the complex Red Pyramid (also at Dashur), and the Meidum Pyramid. To undertake such ambitious building projects Sneferu needed vast supplies of raw materials, not to mention a vast labour force. He probably obtained both by conquering areas of Libya and Nubia and securing a ready supply of slaves, stone and timber to execute and finance his ambitions.

Khufu: a cruel genius?

The second pharaoh of Egypt's Fourth Dynasty, Khufu reigned from c.2589-2566 BC during the period of the Old Kingdom and relatively little is known about him, except that he fathered numerous sons and daughters and had a reputation for cruelty. One achievement, however, secures his place in history: he is generally accepted to be the builder of the Great Pyramid at Giza – the largest single building of ancient times and the pinnacle of the Old Kingdom's splendour.

The Great Pyramid was intended as Khufu's last resting place, but the sarcophagus found during excavations in its King's Chamber was empty. Khufu was doubtless inspired to undertake such an epic construction by the work of his father, Sneferu, the great pyramid-building pioneer.

So was his reputation for cruelty deserved? Historians such as Herodotus have made various accusations against him, claiming that he forced large numbers of slaves to construct the Great Pyramid and that he even prostituted one of his daughters to help finance the building work. But it's now more generally accepted that the Pyramid was built by highly trained craftsmen aided by labourers who were recompensed for their work.

Napoleon and the Great Pyramid

"From the heights of these pyramids, 40 centuries look down on us" – the French emperor Napoleon Bonaparte's rousing words to his troops as he rammed home the Giza pyramids' majestic historical significance.

As part of his rampant imperial expansionism, Napoleon fought a campaign in Egypt from 1798-1801. On 21 July 1798 his army engaged the forces of the Mamluk Turks in what the French emperor would dub 'The Battle of the Pyramids'. (The battle was fought at Embabeh, near Cairo, the Great Pyramid and its mighty companions looming on the horizon some 10 miles away).

Napoleon's involvement in Egypt was not purely military. French scholars and archaeologists travelling with his army studied the country's ancient history and made some important finds, including the Rosetta Stone, which was key in deciphering Egyptian hieroglyphs. The Stone became British property in 1801 when it was handed over as part of the Treaty of Alexandria after Napoleon's defeat in Egypt, and it's now part of the British Museum's collection.

There is a story, possibly apocryphal, that Napoleon visited the King's Chamber in the Great Pyramid and there had an experience so incredible and disturbing that he would never speak of it, not even on his deathbed. As when Alexander the Great consulted the Oracle at the Siwa Oasis, had supernatural forces foretold his destiny?

Flinders Petrie: pyramid pioneer

The British Egyptologist Flinders Petrie (1853-1942) is regarded as the first truly professional Egyptologist. (His grandfather, Matthew Flinders, was famous for mapping the Australian coastline).

Flinders Petrie pioneered a systematic methodology for archaeology and introduced new techniques for excavating, site preservation and recording finds. He made significant discoveries at major sites such as Tanis, Abydos and Amarna and was alarmed by the woeful state of Egypt's great monuments, describing their decay as "like a house on fire, so rapid was the destruction". He reserved a particular contempt for tomb-raiders, whose smash-and-grab techniques destroyed so much of the crucial evidence that could be secured by painstaking, systematic archaeology.

Taking precise measurements was central to Petrie's work, although he was not the first to apply this to the pyramids. In 1646 the British antiquary John Greaves published his Pyramidographia, having journeyed to Egypt and measured various structures. Petrie, a trained surveyor, travelled to Giza in 1880 and was the first to measure the Great Pyramid in detail and to explore its construction, debunking many previous theories.

On his death in 1942, Petrie, apart from his head, was buried in the Protestant cemetery in Jerusalem. His head he donated to the Royal College of Surgeons.

THE HANGING GARDENS OF BABYLON

The Hanging Garden of Babylon, from J.A. Hammerton's Wonders of the Past.

A lush, lavish earthly paradise, a towering structure that seemed to float in the air, the ultimate romantic gesture of a husband to a homesick wife: of all the Seven Wonders of the ancient world, the lost Hanging Gardens of Babylon cast the most potent spell.

But did they actually exist in such spectacular form? Or were they merely an elaborate construct of the poetic imagination, concocted from detailed descriptions passed down through the centuries?

Babylon, ancient city-state

Lost in time and shrouded in myths, ancient Babylon itself seems like a city built by the gods, with its links to so many other 'legendary' people, places and events: the exotic Queen Semiramis, the Tower of Babel, Belshazzar's Feast and the dreaded writing on the wall: "You have been weighed in the balance and found wanting".

Babylon lay in ancient Mesopotamia on the fertile plains by the River Euphrates, a site some 50 miles south of the present day Iraqi capital, Baghdad. A royal city-state, it first came to prominence under the reign of King Hammurabi (c.1792-1750 BC), renowned for organising the laws of Babylonia into the Code of Hammurabi.

Around 1500 BC the city and its surrounding empire fell under the control of the Kassite kings, who came from an area occupied by modern-day Iran and whose dynasty would last for more than 400 years. During this time Babylon grew into a great centre of learning for diverse disciplines, from mathematics and medicine to divination and astrology. At the time it may well have been the largest city on earth, its population a staggering 200,000.

From 911-608 BC the Assyrians ruled the city and were at constant war with the Chaldeans (in 698 BC the city suffered the unfortunate fate of being razed to the ground). The Chaldeans eventually triumphed over the Assyrians, destroying their empire with help from the Persians and Scythians, and from 608-539 BC the city became the centre of a great Babylonian empire.

Under Nebuchadnezzar II (reigned c.605-562 BC), Babylon underwent major rebuilding. Something of a megalomaniac, Nebuchadnezzar rebuilt the grounds of the imperial palace and the city's spectacular gated walls (themselves considered a wonder of the world).

Strabo, the first-century BC historian, takes his description of Babylon and its walls from a fourth-century BC account, now lost:

"Babylon...lies in a plain, and the circuit of its wall is three hundred and eighty-five stadia...and the passage on top of the wall is such that four-horse chariots can easily pass one another. It is on this account that this and the hanging garden are called the Seven Wonders of the World."

But did King Nebuchadnezzar construct the Hanging Gardens, as some have suggested?

A homesick queen

There are no known first-hand accounts of the Hanging Gardens of Babylon. Like Strabo, several writers of antiquity quote earlier sources such as Berossus, a Babylonian priest who lived in the fourth century BC.

Berossus did credit Nebuchadnezzar with building the gardens. His writings also support the belief that the gardens were a gift for Nebuchadnezzar's wife, Amytis, daughter or granddaughter of King Cyaxares of Media. Nebuchadnezzar was said to have built the Hanging Gardens to assuage Amytis' homesickness for the mountainous landscape of her homeland.

"In this place," writes Berossus, "he [Nebuchadnezzar] erected very high walks supported by stone pillars, and by planting what he called a pensile paradise and replenishing it with all sorts of trees, he rendered the prospect an exact resemblance of a mountainous country. He did this to gratify his queen, because she was brought up in Media and was fond of its mountainous landscape."

Quoting the early fourth-century BC texts of Ctesias of Cnidus, the first-century BC historian

Diodorus Siculus echoes this story, although he refers not to a wife but to a concubine. He states:

"There was also...the Hanging Garden, as it is called, which was built not by Semiramis but by a later Syrian king to please one of his concubines. For she, they say, being a Persian by race and longing for the meadows of the mountains, asked the king to imitate the distinctive landscape of Persia through the artifice of a planted garden."

But what did the Hanging Gardens actually look like?

Diodorus Siculus again:

"...since the approach to the garden sloped like a hillside and several parts of the structure rose tier on tier, the whole resembled a theatre."

Philo of Byzantium (c.250 BC), writes:

"This is a work of royal luxury, and its most striking feature is that the labour of cultivation is suspended above the heads of the spectators."

He continues:

"It is filled with all sorts of trees and looks exactly like mountain country, and several parts of it grow one on another to resemble a theatre. It is thickly planted, and the trees' broad leaves almost touch each other and make delightful shade. Waters gush forth from high fountains and sink down to the ground and are forced up again in twists and spirals, rushing and swirling through the pipes. Bountiful moisture bathes the trees and the soil is perpetually moist."

The writings of Strabo provide further details:

"The garden is quadrangular in shape...it consists of arched vaults, which are situated, one after another, on chequered cube-lie foundations. The foundations, which are hollowed out, are covered so deep with earth that they allow the largest of trees..."

Siculus gives details of planting, writing that:

"earth had been piled to a depth sufficient for the roots of the largest trees, and the ground, when levelled off, was thickly planted with trees of every kind that, by their great size or other charm, could give pleasure to the beholder."

Many were struck by the ingenious use of large Archimedes screws, which can propel water uphill and which were employed to water the Hanging Gardens. "The ascent to the uppermost terraces is made by a stairway," writes Strabo, "and alongside these stairs there were screws through which the water was continually conducted up to the garden from the Euphrates by those appointed for this purpose."

Downfall of a legendary city

In 539 BC the last Babylonian king, Nabonidus, was defeated and the empire fell to Cyrus the Great, the king of Persia. He entered the supposedly impenetrable city of Babylon on the night of a great feast (which probably formed the basis for the feast of Belshazzar as related in the Bible in the Book of Daniel). His mode of entry was ingenious. Cyrus' troops diverted the adjacent Euphrates, lowering the level of the river so that they could enter via security gates that were normally under water.

Babylon continued to flourish under Persian kings such as Darius the Great. In 331 BC Darius III was defeated by Alexander the Great and once more Babylon became a great centre of learning. Alexander famously died in the city in 323 BC, and in the years of turmoil that followed Babylon went into decline and was struck by several earthquakes.

For countless centuries Babylon remained as little more than a pile of rubble. Various archaeologists have excavated the site and claim to have found the possible location of the Hanging Gardens. From 1899 up to the start of the First World War the German archaeologist Robert Koldewey systematically explored Babylon and believed that he had found the Gardens' foundations, but they proved to be nothing more than municipal offices. Some believe the Hanging Gardens may not even be in Babylon, but were actually built in the ancient Assyrian capital of Nineveh.

In 1983 the Iraqi leader Saddam Hussein began to reconstruct Babylon over the ruins of the ancient city. Saddam considered himself the reincarnation of Nebuchadnezzar and, like the Babylonian king, inscribed the bricks with his own name. His downfall halted the project.

Whether myth or reality, the Hanging Gardens inspired a wealth of imitations down the centuries, from the fabulous Renaissance gardens of the Villa d'Este, near Rome, to the vogue for the elaborate 'hanging gardens' that adorn various 'designer' homes and multi-storeyed structures in today's towns and cities.

Nebuchadnezzar II, creator of the Hanging Gardens?

His egregious exploits are covered in detail in the Bible – Nebuchadnezzar, the Babylonian king who conquered Judah and Jerusalem, destroyed the First Temple, and sent the Jews into exile.

He was the son of Nabopolassar, who had liberated Babylon from the Assyrians. He reigned from c.605-562 BC, marrying Amytis of Media in a political move to unite Babylonia with the powerful Median Empire. Having conquered Judah, Nebuchadnezzar conquered Jerusalem in 597 BC, destroying the city during a rebellion a decade later.

In Babylon, Nebuchadnezzar's influence was literally more constructive. He made the city a glorious object, sparing no expense in completing the royal palace with decor featuring "bronze, gold, silver, rare and precious stones". He may also, at this time, have created the Hanging Gardens.

The Bible portrays Nebuchadnezzar as a proud king and idolater humbled by God. It also portrays him as a man stricken by insanity. The prophet Daniel interprets a dream that troubles Nebuchadnezzar as a prophecy – a prophecy that he will go mad and wander the wilderness for seven years. The Book of Daniel also describes Nebuchadnezzar as an idolater who cast the three Jews, Shadrach, Meshach and Abednego, into the Burning Fiery Furnace when they refused to bow down and worship the vast gold idol he'd created. They were said to have been protected by a fourth presence, a fiery angel resembling the 'son of God', and emerged from the flames unscathed.

Do these Biblical references relate to actual events in Nebuchadnezzar's life? It's possible. Some scholars have referenced evidence of mental instability, which might be the product of either monomania or diseases such as porphyria or syphilis.

Queen Semiramis

Another possible candidate as creator of the Hanging Gardens (although a much less likely one) is the legendary Assyrian queen, Semiramis.

Semiramis herself seems little more than a myth. Legends claim that she was queen to King Ninus, succeeding him to become ruler of Assyria. Others that she may have been the real-life Shammuramat, queen of Shamshi-Ada V, king of Assyria, who ruled from c.824-811 BC.

Whether myth or reality, according to the writers of the ancient world who recorded her exploits, such as Diodorus Siculus, Semiramis was a goddess-like creature and responsible for building virtually every major marvel of antiquity. Some believe her to be half-god, half-mortal, the offspring of the fish-goddess Derketo of Ascalon who abandoned her to be raised by Simmas, a royal shepherd. Rising to become wife of King Ninus of Assyria, Semiramis ruled as regent after his death, building the high brick walls that protected Babylon.

Other legends are less benign, portraying Semiramis as vengeful and lustful, not to mention a sorceress, who led armies against a man who'd spurned her advances and, when he was slain in battle, tried to raise him from the dead. Diodorus confidently claims that Semiramis was not the creator of the Hanging Gardens, but her cultural legacy lives on, inspiring Dante to condemn her to the Second Circle of Hell in The Divine Comedy and classical composers as diverse as Rossini and Honegger to immortalise her through music.

Etemenanki and the Tower of Babel

Just as various sites of the ancient world gave rise to the possible 'myth' of Babylon's great Hanging Gardens, did the Ziggurat of Etemenanki at Babylon inspire the Biblical story of the Tower of Babel?

What became known as the Tower of Babel – a vast structure spiralling up high into the sky, whose inhabitants spoke in a babble of tongues – is mentioned in the Book of Genesis. Genesis 11:4 states "And they said, Go to, let us build us a city and a tower, whose top may reach unto heaven."

The astonishing structure of the ziggurat of Etemenanki (meaning 'temple of the foundations of heaven and earth'), built in Babylon in the sixth century BC, may have been the inspiration for the Biblical story of the Tower.

Archaeological evidence may also point to Nebuchadnezzar II as the builder of the ziggurat, a multi-tiered temple bearing an inscription found in 1917 that states

"...I made it, the wonder of the people of the world, I raised its top to heaven."

In 440 BC the historian Herodotus makes reference to a similarly imposing structure at Babylon, which may well have been the ziggurat. He describes it as

"...a tower of solid masonry...upon which was raised a second tower, and on that a third...and so on up to eight. The ascent to the top is on the outside, by a path that winds up around all the towers."

Whatever the facts of the matter, the ziggurat of Etemenanki fell into disrepair and began to collapse. Alexander the Great ordered that it be rebuilt when he conquered Babylon in 331 BC. When he returned to the city in 323 BC – the year of his death – little progress had been made and he ordered its demolition.

THE TEMPLE OF ARTEMIS AT EPHESUS

An engraving of the Temple of Artemis at Ephesus by Fischer von Erlach, c. 1721.

"I have set eyes on the wall of lofty Babylon along which chariots race, and the statue of Zeus by the Alpheus, and the hanging gardens, and the Colossus of Helios, and the huge labour of the high pyramids, and the vast tomb of Mausolus, but when I saw the house of Artemis that mounted to the clouds, those other marvels lost their brilliancy, and I said: 'Behold, apart from Olympus, the Sun never looked on anything so grand'."

So wrote Antipater of Sidon, one of the compilers of the Seven Wonders list, of the Temple of Artemis at Ephesus.

From its acoustically perfect Theatre to the Library of Celsus, which must be one of the most beautiful surviving structures of antiquity, even today, some 15 centuries after the Temple of Artemis was buried by the sands, Ephesus is truly a city of wonders.

The cult of Artemis

Its history is both long and rich and dates back to a thousand years before the birth of Christ. According to some, its mythological founder was Ephos, Queen of the Amazons, and after being sacked by warring tribes it was rebuilt in the sixth century BC by an equally resonant name: the fabulously wealthy Croesus, king of the Lydians. Persians, Greeks and Romans made their mark on the city over succeeding centuries, and in the mid-first century AD it became an important centre for Early Christianity and the home of Saints Paul and John the Apostle. It was even, some believe, the final earthly residence of the Virgin Mary.

The ancient monuments of Ephesus, which lies close to the town of Selçuk in modern-day Turkey, have made the city one of the most famous international tourist destinations of the Eastern Mediterranean. But little remains of what is, perhaps, its most celebrated monument: the

Temple of Artemis, one of the Seven Wonders of the World. Indeed, for centuries its remains lay buried beneath some 25 feet of sand until the 1860s, when its foundations were located by the British archaeologist John Turtle Wood.

Dedicated to Artemis, goddess of the hunt, fertility and childbirth, the Temple had a turbulent history and was destroyed and rebuilt on numerous occasions. There may have been a temple on the site as far back as the Bronze Age, where the ancient tribes of the area would have worshipped early pagan deities which evolved into the gods of Ancient Greece and then Ancient Rome. Legend even has it that the site provided sanctuary for the Amazons as they fled from the unwanted attentions of rampant male gods, such as Dionysus.

The riches of Croesus – and a notorious act of arson

A temple that stood on the site was destroyed by a flood in the seventh century BC. In c.550 BC, King Croesus, king of the Lydians and overlord of Ephesus, financed the Temple's reconstruction, the architects said to be Chersiphron and his son

Metagenes. It was a colossal structure built of marble, some 377 feet long by 151 feet wide, its great forest of columns soaring to a height of 40 feet. Just as thousands flock to Ephesus today to enjoy its marvels, in antiquity the Temple became a place of pilgrimage for those who wished to make offerings to the cult of 'Artemisia Ephesia' – Artemis of Ephesus – whose votive statue stood in the Temple's inner sanctum.

Then, in 356 BC, the year of the birth of Alexander the Great, came one of history's most notorious acts of arson. Staged purely to ensure his 'immortality', a man named Herostratus set fire to the roof beams of the Temple and it burned to the ground. The city's authorities punished Herostratus not merely by executing him, but also by forbidding in perpetuity any mention of his name on pain of death. The news of Herostratus' exploits leaked out, however, courtesy of the historian Theopompus. The term 'Herostratic fame' is still used today to denote an outrageous criminal act committed merely to attain fame at any cost.

An offer from Alexander

Alexander the Great himself was eager to finance the rebuilding of the Temple, but the Ephesians, being peculiarly independent types, politely but firmly declined his offer. Construction of a new Temple began in 323 BC, the year of Alexander's death, and this version was on a scale even greater than that financed by Croesus. It was 450 feet long, 225 feet wide and 60 feet high, and many writers of antiquity, such as Pliny the Elder, recorded seeing inside the Temple magnificent sculptures and carved reliefs, columns gilded with silver and gold, and a great main cult image of the Temple's dedicatee, Artemis, adorned with necklaces that resembled multiple swags of breasts (her image, the Lady of Ephesus, can be found in the city's museum).

Former versions of the Temple had fallen victim to floods and an arsonist. It was Christians, Goths and then the plundering of the Temple's remaining masonry for use elsewhere that finally destroyed this Temple of Artemis, although it did survive for about 600 years.

Romans and Christians

Shortly before the birth of Christ, Ephesus enjoyed another surge in its fortunes when it became part of the Roman Republic. The first ruler of the Roman Empire, Augustus, who became emperor in 27 BC, made Ephesus the capital of Roman Asia. Now second in size and importance only to Rome, it expanded into an even more prosperous city with a population that may have reached half a million. The Theatre, which had staged Greek drama, now became an arena for the gory Roman spectacle of gladiatorial combat (one of Ephesus' archaeological sites is a gladiators' graveyard). The Roman belief system also took hold in the city, the Temple of Artemis becoming the Temple of Diana, the goddess' Roman equivalent deity.

Then another religion spread its influence in the city. From the mid-first century AD Ephesus became a major centre for Early Christianity. Christ's disciple St. Paul lived there from AD 52-54 and preached in the Theatre, encountering a certain amount of resistance as he urged the citizens to shun their pagan gods and turn to the teachings of Jesus Christ.

St. John the Apostle is also believed to have spent his final years in Ephesus and to be buried on the slope of the Ayosolug Hill. St. John is traditionally credited with writing both the Gospel of John and the Book of Revelations, in which Ephesus is referred to as one of the seven churches of Asia, and there is even an apocryphal tale that St. John brought about the Temple's destruction and converted the Ephesians to Christianity. Tradition also has it that the Virgin Mary spent her final years in Ephesus.

In the sixth decade of the third century, the Temple was severely damaged when Ephesus was sacked by the Goths. But once again the city rose, phoenix-like, under the rule of Constantine (reigned AD 306-337), the first Christian emperor of Rome and founder of the capital of the Byzantine Empire, Constantinople. Little is known from this era of the Temple's fate. Constantine and his successors may have rebuilt it, but it's thought that some of its columns were reused in the mighty Byzantine church of Hagia Sophia in Constantinople (modern-day Istanbul).

Two greats of British archaeology

In due course, what little remained of the Temple of Artemis became buried, its location lost until the 1860s.

Two prominent British archaeologists of the nineteenth century were responsible both for its rediscovery and detailed excavation. For John Turtle Wood (1821-90), who was also an architect and engineer, the rediscovery of the Temple's precise location became a lifelong obsession and one conducted at great personal risk from such perils as disease, earthquakes and bandits.

John Romer's accompanying documentary traces in illuminating detail the means by which Wood was able to track down the Temple's precise location following the discovery of a vital inscription in the theatre at Ephesus. Romer describes what happened next as the most romantic archaeological search ever mounted. Despairing of ever finding the Temple, Wood's problems increased further when he broke his foot. It proved to be the most fortunate of accidents. Wood's wife Elizabeth, who was also an archaeologist, was able to take over the excavations under her husband's supervision, and on the very last day of 1869 they uncovered a marble pavement from the Temple some 25 feet down.

Wood transported various fragments from the Temple back to London where they were given to the British Museum, which had helped to fund his expedition to Ephesus. Further excavations were conducted from 1904-06 by the archaeologist and scholar David George Hogarth (1862-1927), who was able to add further pieces to the Ephesus collection at the British Museum. Hogarth is also known for his association with Lawrence of Arabia when he headed the Arab Bureau in Cairo during the First World War. He worked as keeper at Oxford's Ashmolean Museum from 1909 until his death.

Croesus, king of an economic revolution

In Ancient Greek and Persian cultures the name of Croesus was synonymous with riches, and the phrase "As rich as Croesus" is still used today to denote wealth on an exceptional scale.

Croesus has almost passed into myth, but from c.560-547 BC he was king of Lydia, a powerful realm in modern-day western Turkey, its territory embracing the city of Ephesus, where Croesus financed the rebuilding of the Temple of Artemis in c.550 BC. In Sardis, the wealthy and sophisticated city that was the capital of his kingdom, he also brought about an economic revolution by essentially 'inventing' a standardised form of money.

This came about from local mineral deposits. The 'golden sands' of the River Pactolus, which flowed down through the mountains to Sardis, were in fact gold dust mixed with the river's alluvial deposits. From this Croesus was able to mint gold coins of exceptional purity that had a set value.

Within 50 years, Sardis, already an important trade hub, had spawned a great industry of smelting workshops, banks and moneylenders, which rapidly spread beyond the kingdom's boundaries.

Lydia eventually fell to Cyrus the Great of Persia, who took Croesus captive in Sardis. According to legend, Cyrus placed the living Croesus on a great funeral pyre, to see if the gods would intervene and save him from being burned alive. Before the flames could envelop him, Croesus is said to have been snatched to safety by the god Apollo. Another version of the story claims that Cyrus repented of such brutality and ordered the flames to be extinguished before Croesus was burned to a crisp.

Artemis, goddess and huntress

According to Greek mythology, Artemis was the daughter of Zeus, king of the gods, and the goddess Leto. She was also the twin of the god Apollo.

While still a girl, Artemis begged her father Zeus to grant her eternal chastity and to give her a bow and arrows, so that she might enjoy the pleasures of the hunt – her symbols are the crescent moon, the stag, the bear, the bow and arrow, and the hunting dog. She also asked for 20 nymphs as hunting companions, all of them to be virgins too.

Artemis (Diana in the Roman pantheon) was very protective of her chastity and dealt ruthlessly with male admirers who overstepped the mark.

One of her most celebrated acts of revenge was against Actaeon, who chanced upon Artemis and her handmaidens bathing naked at a secluded pool and made inappropriate advances. In revenge, Artemis had Actaeon turned into a stag and he was torn apart by his hounds.

The only true love of her life was Orion, her hunting companion, whom she was tricked into killing by her brother, Apollo. After his death, Orion became a constellation, with Sirius, the trusty 'dog-star', as his companion.

As with many of the gods, Artemis had contradictory attributes. She was the protector of women in childbirth but her arrows could also kill those in labour, and she could spread disease as well as exercise healing powers. At Ephesus she was worshipped primarily as a fertility goddess rather than as a goddess-huntress, her cult image as Artemisia Ephesia, with its curious pendulous breast-like adornments, worshipped at her temple. She was held in high esteem by the local populace. A Biblical text states how they chanted "Great is Artemis of the Ephesians!"

when St. Paul attempted to ban 'pagan' representations of the goddess from the city.

THE STATUE OF ZEUS AT OLYMPIA

An undated print of the Statue of Zeus at Olympia.

Olympia: earthly sanctuary of the Greek gods, birthplace of the Olympic Games and the site of one of the most awesome statues in history.

The colossal statue of Zeus, king of the Greek gods, dominated the temple that was built for it in the Altis, or sanctuary, at Olympia, its startling presence occupying half the width of the aisle and reaching as high as the rafters of the temple roof. Equally legendary is the name of the man who created it: Phidias, regarded as one of the greatest sculptors of antiquity. His statue of Zeus was the grandest single figure of Ancient Greece, positioned at the spiritual heart of Greek culture.

Ivory, gold and jewels

Created c.430-422 BC, the seated figure towered to about 42 feet. Its wooden framework was plated with a skin made of polished ivory and robes and sandals of gold, all embellished with precious stones. This chryselephantine statue sat on an elaborate cedar-wood throne, similarly embellished. A single glimpse of the statue was said to make a man forget all his troubles, and the ancient writer Strabo observed that had it stood up it would have literally raised the roof. Philo of Byzantium, that vital witness of the Seven Wonders, remarked: "The other six wonders we honour, but Zeus we venerate."

The name Olympia describes the wooded valley where the site is located in the area of Greece known as Peloponnesus. Its name referred to the sacred mountain of Olympus, the residence of Zeus. It had been a centre for the worship of this king of the gods since the tenth century BC, as evidenced by the remains of food and burnt offerings found at the site.

The elaborate complex known as the Altis developed over the centuries, and in the eighth century BC it became famous as the site for the first Olympic Games, which attracted athletes and spectators from all over Greece. It expanded to contain one of the highest concentrations of artistic masterpieces in the ancient Mediterranean world.

An order from Caligula

The two main temples of the sanctuary were the sixth-century BC Temple of Hera, and the Temple of Zeus, constructed 470-457 BC, its majestic form a model for numerous later temples across the Mediterranean and a showcase for Phidias' masterpiece. In the second century AD the writer Pausanias provided a detailed description of the statue's appearance, and noted than in Zeus' right hand was a small statue of Nike, the goddess of victory. Pausanias also wrote:

"On his head is a sculpted wreath of olive sprays...In his left hand he holds a sceptre inlaid with every kind of metal, with an eagle perched on the sceptre."

Various stories surround the statue's eventual destruction. It's said that the notorious Roman emperor Caligula (AD 12-41) ordered that its head should be removed and replaced with his own image. Some say it was destroyed along with the temple in a fire in AD 425, others that it was carried off to Constantinople where it was destroyed in a later fire in AD 475, its powerful image eventually adopted in Christian iconography as the seated Christ in majesty.

Cradle of the Olympics

The ancient Olympic Games epitomised the noble Hellenistic ideal of peaceful competition between free and equal men prepared to push themselves to the height of physical achievement – and all for the humble symbolic reward of an olive wreath.

From 776 BC to AD 395, the Games were held at Olympia every four years in honour of Zeus, king of the gods. They attracted crowds of up to 50,000 to watch an array of sports that grew over the centuries, starting with nothing more than a humble running race and eventually offering a wide range of spectacles including discus and javelin throwing, the long jump, boxing, wrestling, chariot racing and the pankration – essentially a brutal 'contact sport'.

The Games were conducted under what was known as the 'Sacred Truce', a month-long cessation of hostilities that forced the warring city-states of Greece to put aside their differences for the duration of the Games.

But they were not just a sports festival: they also had deep religious significance, with athletes making offerings to Zeus to win his favour. If caught cheating, they had to pay a fine that was used to make a cult statue of the god. Women were not allowed to participate in the main Games (or even, possibly, to watch), but had their own games in honour of Zeus' wife, the goddess Hera.

The ancient Olympic Games continued until they were banned by the Christian Byzantine emperor Theodosius I in the fourth century AD. They formed the model, however, for the modern Olympics, which were revived in 1896. Prior to each modern Games, the Olympic flame is lit from the rays of the sun by a parabolic mirror at a special ceremony held at Olympia.

Phidias, creative genius...and thief?

One of the most exciting archaeological discoveries at Olympus was not the treasures of the sanctuary but the workshop where the sculptor Phidias fashioned the statue of Zeus. Unearthed in the mid-1950s, it still contained the tools used by the master-sculptor and even a cup bearing the legend "I belong to Phidias".

Phidias (c.480-430 BC) also produced the monumental statues of Athena Pathenos and Athena Promachos at the Parthenon in Athens, and was commissioned to make several sculptures for the Athenian statesman Pericles. As with so many other Greek masterpieces, the serene works of Phidias are known only from later copies, the originals having been lost.

Phidias is said to have based his portrayal of Zeus on the description given in Homer's epic, the Illiad. He also appears to have been somewhat light-fingered. John Romer notes in his book on the Seven Wonders of the World that Phidias was accused, both in Athens and Olympia, of stealing some of the precious metals associated with the statues, although he may have been the innocent victim of a conspiracy.

Zeus, seducer in disguise

His symbols are the thunderbolt, the eagle, the bull and the oak. To the Greeks, he was the king of the gods, who oversaw the universe. To his wife Hera he was constantly unfaithful, incurring her wrath while fathering an impressive line of offspring, including Athena, Apollo, Artemis, Aphrodite, Hermes, Persephone, Dionysus, Perseus, Heracles and Helen of Troy.

According to various myths, Zeus resorted to ingenious but devious means to seduce unwilling or unwitting females. He could adopt disguises with an inventiveness that wouldn't disgrace a modern-day superhero (or super-villain), impregnating Danae, for example, in the form of a shower of golden rain. This resulted in the birth of their son Perseus.

Zeus adopted the form of a swan to seduce Leda. The nymph Callisto, however, escaped his attentions when he tried to seduce this resolute virgin in the form of his own daughter Artemis. She was transformed into a bear and became the constellation Ursa Minor.

THE MAUSOLEUM AT HALICARNASSUS

Apart from the Great Pyramid at Giza, little remains of the Seven Wonders of the World. There are no known extant physical remnants for the Hanging Gardens of Babylon, their breathtaking scale and enchanting beauty surviving only in secondhand descriptions by various historians of antiquity, and fragments of sculpture and masonry or just piles of rubble are all that is left of the other five Wonders.

But some fragments are more impressive than others, and a visitor to the British Museum confronted with the remains of a monumental horse (still with its original bronze bridle) that was one of four that once topped the Mausoleum of Halicarnassus, can appreciate something of the magnificence and colossal scale of this ancient tomb. In another room at the British Museum you can also see a reconstruction of the exquisite Nereid Monument from Xanthos, whose raised, tiered structure and decorative statues possibly inspired the Mausoleum's design.

A curious love match

The Mausoleum of Halicarnassus was built c.353-350 BC for Mausolus, a satrap (provincial governor) of the Persian Empire, and his wife Artemesia. Interestingly, Artemisia was also Mausolus' sister. The pair ruled over the small state of Caria, the capital of which was the coastal city of Halicarnassus (the modern-day Turkish city of Bodrum), and Mausolus' name gave rise to the term 'mausoleum', now used generically to describe any large, stately commemorative tomb. Halicarnassus was also the birthplace of Herodotus (c.484-425 BC), the writer known as the 'father of history' for his precise methodology and vivid narratives.

Lovers of all things Greek, Mausolus and Artemesia spent a vast amount of public money embellishing their capital with splendid temples and statues, along with a palace and theatre. On Mausoleus' death in 353 BC his grieving widow commissioned a tomb of exceptional magnificence to perpetuate his memory, recruiting the most eminent Greek architects and sculptors to design its overall appearance and create the great statues and reliefs so that the building would be "adorned in men and horses carved as if they were real and in fine marble".

Those who worked on the Mausoleum were the architects Satyros and Pythius (who designed buildings at the imposing city of Priene) and the sculptors Leochares, Bryaxis, Scopas of Paros and Timotheus, each carving the figures for one of the four sides of the structure.

Hovering on a silver cloud

Descriptions of the Mausoleum's appearance have come down to us through the writings of ancient authors such as Pausanias, Strabo, Vitruvius, Hyginus and Pliny the Elder. It was erected on a hilltop overlooking Halicarnassus and was enclosed within a courtyard. Pliny the Elder reports that the main body of the tomb was slightly rectangular rather than square. It was positioned on a broad stone platform, each side about 60-70 feet in length, its upper section decorated with 36 slim columns enclosing a smaller block that supported the tomb's massive pyramidal roof.

The entire structure stood about 148 feet high, and perched on the apex of the pyramid was a quadriga of four massive horses pulling a chariot of bronze and marble in which rode images of

Mausolus and Artemisia. It was a spectacular sight, said to hang over the city as if hovering on a silver cloud, and probably stood over Halicarnassus for some sixteen centuries until a series of earthquakes reduced its superstructure to a ragged pile of masonry. By 1404 only the base remained relatively intact. Even less remained when the site of the Mausoleum was rediscovered by the British archaeologist Charles Newton in 1856-57.

Artemisia II of Caria, a devoted wife and sister

The tomb chamber of the Mausoleum at Halicarnassus suffered the fate of so many such monuments of antiquity and fell prey to grave robbers, although Mausolus and Artemesia were most likely cremated, the Mausoleum containing nothing more than their ashes.

Artemisia was the wife, sister and successor of Mausolus, ruler of Caria. Renowned for her deep and enduring grief on the death of her husband, she is said to have mixed his ashes into liquid and drunk the resulting potion on a daily basis.

Following Mausolus' death she also ruled the country single-handedly as well as commissioning the monument that would preserve their memory for eternity. Artemisia never lived to see it completed, pining away from grief and dying two years after her husband.

Charles Newton and the thrill of discovery

The pinpointing of the location of the ruined Mausoleum of Halicarnassus was the high point of archaeologist Charles Newton's career.

Born in 1816, in 1840 he joined the staff of the British Museum's Antiquities Department. Financed by Lord Stratford de Redcliffe, the British ambassador in Constantinople, in the 1850s Newton began archaeological excavations along the coast of Asia Minor, and in 1856-57 he made his landmark discovery at Halicarnassus, including the fragments of the monumental horse now in the British Museum.

Some of the thrill of Newton's discovery of the monumental statues at the site is conveyed in his own description of the event:

"After being duly hauled out, [the horse] was placed on a sledge and dragged to the shore by 80 Turkish workmen. On the walls and housetops as we went along sat the veiled ladies of Bodrum. They had never seen anything so big before, and the sight overcame the reserve placed on them by Turkish etiquette. The ladies of Troy gazing down on the Wooden Horse as he entered the breach could not have been more astonished."

Charles Newton's finds at Halicarnassus were among those conveyed to the British Museum. A diplomat as well as an archaeologist, he was appointed British consul to Rome in 1860, but he gave up this post almost immediately to return to the Museum, where he set about the re-organisation of the Greek and Roman section and the building of the Mausoleum Room to house the Halicarnassus treasures.

Newton was also active in the founding and running of the Society for the Promotion of Hellenic Studies, the British School in Athens and the Egypt Exploration Fund. In 1861 he married Ann Mary Severn, the daughter of the painter

Joseph Severn, who as a young man had accompanied his friend, the dying poet John Keats, on his final tragic journey to Rome. Charles Newton died in Margate in 1894.

THE COLOSSUS OF RHODES

Maerten van Heemskerck's 16th century coloured engraving of the Colossus of Rhodes.

A massive bronze god, over one hundred feet high and straddling a harbour mouth, flaming torch held aloft, the masts of great ships passing between his legs: this is the classic image of the wonder of the ancient world known as the Colossus of Rhodes, a masterpiece of both art and engineering.

The reality was no doubt impressive but somewhat different. It's highly unlikely that the Colossus straddled a harbour mouth as a statue on such a scale built of bronze would have simply collapsed under its own weight. The image is most likely a fanciful product of the literary imagination (in Shakespeare's Julius Caesar, for example, Cassius says of Caesar that "...he doth bestride the narrow world like a Colossus, and we petty men walk under his huge legs".)

Born of warfare and gratitude

What is known is that the Colossus was built in the city of Rhodes on the Greek island of the same name between 292 and 280 BC. Its architect was Chares of Lindos, and it was one of the tallest statues of the ancient world. It stood for little more than 60 years before being felled by an earthquake in 226 BC.

The Colossus of Rhodes was the product of warfare and gratitude. A mercantile republic with a large and vigorous navy, the Eastern Mediterranean island had grown rich on the harbour dues derived from the vast amount of trade that passed through its port. It effectively controlled the entrance to the Aegean and had great strategic importance, which made it an attractive target for those who wished to seize Rhodes' power and influence for their own ends.

The Siege of Rhodes of 305-304 BC is one of the most famous of antiquity. It was staged by the Macedonian Demetrius Poliorcetes, the son of

Alexander the Great's successor and general, Antigonus I, to break the island's alliance with Ptolemy I of Egypt. Demetrius had already conquered Cyprus in 306 BC, but Rhodes proved more resilient. Backed up by Ptolemy's naval forces, for a year the city withstood Demetrius' blockade and he was forced to settle the conflict with a peace treaty.

Demetrius' forces withdrew, leaving behind much of their siege machinery, including a large metal siege tower known as the Helepolis. Through melting down or selling off this paraphernalia of war, the citizens of Rhodes were able to celebrate their liberation by using it to fund a mighty commemorative statue of their patron god, Helios, whose cult prevailed on the island.

A tribute to a god

For an architect they turned to Chares of Lindos, a native of the island who had experience of building largescale statues (he was a pupil of Lysippos, court sculptor to Alexander the Great, who'd constructed a 70-foot bronze statue of Zeus at Tarentum). The site chosen for the Colossus was most likely to one side of the entrance to the Mandraki Harbour, possibly on a breakwater. The Colossus itself was about 98 feet high and stood on a 50 foot-high platform of white marble. The lower core of the Colossus was filled with stone to aid stability, its 'skin' formed from bronze plates riveted onto an internal network of iron bars. Earthen mounds were probably built up around the Colossus to aid its construction as it grew in height.

The Colossus was dedicated to Helios, the sun-god of Greek mythology. He is usually portrayed wearing a golden oriole of sunrays on his head, and the Colossus may well have worn the same embellishment. It's 'reign' over the harbour at Rhodes was brief, however – indeed it had the briefest lifespan of any of the Seven Wonders. In 226 BC, a strong earthquake hit the island, destroying much of its capital. According to Strabo, the Colossus snapped at the knees and crashed to earth. The island's ally, Ptolemy III of Egypt, offered funds for its immediate reconstruction but, warned by an oracle not to rebuild the Colossus, the citizens of Rhodes declined his offer.

An ignominious end

For nearly nine centuries, the remains of the Colossus lay on the ground. Even in its fallen, broken state it could still provoke awe. "But even lying on the ground it is a marvel," wrote Pliny the Elder, who also noted that "few people can make their arms meet around the thumb".

In the seventh century, the remains of the Colossus were finally broken up. An Arab force invaded Rhodes and captured the island. According to the chronicler Theophanes the Confessor, the Colossus was "sold to a Jewish merchant from Edessa", who transported his spoils to Syria on the backs of 900 camels, a sad and ignominious end for one of the Wonders of the World.

Master and pupil: Lysippos and Chares of Lindos

Along with Scopas of Paros and Praxiteles, Lysippos is considered to be one of the three greatest sculptors of the Classical Greek era. As with so much Greek sculpture, his work is known only from later copies.

Born around 390 BC, Lysippos worked in both bronze and marble and was known for the grace and elegance of his style, wonderfully apparent in sculptures such as Eros Stringing his Bow (a copy of which can be seen in the British Museum). As court sculptor to Alexander the Great, he produced the images by which we know one of the greatest figures of history, who is usually portrayed as a handsome, vivacious young man with tousled hair. A bronze representation of Alexander by Lysippos was said to have "the look of fire in its eyes".

Like many major sculptors of antiquity Lysippos ran a busy workshop and tutored a large number of pupils, among them Chares of Lindos, the creator of the Colossus of Rhodes. It's possible that Chares did not live long enough to see his statue finished. A story states that he offered to build a statue twice the size of that initially proposed for twice the fee. He failed to calculate, unfortunately, that this would result in an eight-fold increase in material costs, which drove him into bankruptcy and possibly to suicide.

Helios, the sun god

He rose each day from the sea and drove his four-horsed sun chariot across the heavens, encircling the Earth until, at sunset, he plunged back into the waves, heralding the onset of night.

Often identified with Apollo, the Greek god of light, unlike Apollo Helios was not an Olympian. He was a Titan, an older pantheon of ferociously powerful deities descended from the earth (in the form of Gaia) and the sky (in the form of Uranus) who ruled during the Golden Age and were vanquished by the Olympians. One of the best known stories surrounding Helios involved the vainglorious exploits of his son, Phaeton, who famously tried to drive his father's chariot but lost control, crashing to earth and setting the world ablaze.

Did the face of the Colossus of Rhodes reflect that of Alexander the Great? A carved marble head of Helios in the museum at Rhodes certainly resembles, in its facial features and vivacity, depictions of Alexander that survive from the ancient world. It's also been posited that the image of Helios, with his sunray headdress, metamorphosed in later centuries into depictions of the haloed Christ.

'Colossal' inspiration: The Statue of Liberty

The Seven Wonders of the World have inspired countless imitations, great and small, throughout history, and the Colossus of Rhodes was certainly echoed in the design, posture and dimensions of one of the most famous monumental statues of the modern era: the Statue of Liberty in New York Harbour.

Designed by Frédéric Bartholdi and dedicated in 1886, the statue, one arm holding aloft a flaming torch, stands on Liberty Island and welcomed the vast numbers of immigrants who flocked to a new life in the Land of the Free. "Send these, the homeless, tempest-tost to me/I lift my lamp beside the golden door!" states Emma Lazarus' celebrated poem The New Colossus (1883), which is inscribed on a bronze plaque on the Statue. Her poem also makes a less complimentary reference to the Colossus of Rhodes as the "brazen giant of Greek fame".

THE LIGHTHOUSE AT ALEXANDRIA

For centuries probably the tallest manmade structure on earth, the Lighthouse at Alexandria was also one of the most enduring of the Seven Wonders, standing tall for almost 1,500 years before a succession of earthquakes brought much of its mighty height crashing down.

It was said to reach to a height of 300 feet (some estimate it was much higher – possibly 450 feet). It was also one of the earliest known lighthouses in history. Fires on hills and cliffs had been used previously as beacons to warn shipping of coastal hazards, but with the development of major ports the fires became raised onto high platforms to mark the entrance to a harbour. In time, these makeshift platforms became towers of stone.

The Lighthouse at Alexandria is also known as the Pharos of Alexandria, taking its name from the small island of Pharos, which lay just off the coast of Egypt, close to the western side of the Nile Delta – the site that Alexander the Great chose for the eponymous city, which would become the capital for the Ptolemaic rulers of Egypt.

Alexander the Great and the Ptolemaic Dynasty

Founded by Alexander in 331 BC, Alexandria quickly rose to become one of the greatest cities of the world. But even before Alexander conquered Egypt in 332 BC, the Greeks were well established in the Nile delta region.

Around 671 BC the powerful Assyrians attacked Egypt, eventually occupying Memphis and sacking the temples at Thebes. Greek mercenaries helped the Saite pharaohs (who effectively ruled as vassals) to oust their Assyrian masters, and settled in the delta region. In 525 BC the Persians began their conquest of Egypt – an annexation that, despite brief shows of resistance by the Egyptian people, continued until 332 BC when Alexander the Great defeated the Persians and seized power.

Having ousted the hated Persians, Alexander was welcomed in Egypt as a saviour. He was proclaimed the son of the god Amun and his advent ushered in the rule of the Greek Ptolemaic dynasty established by his general Ptolemy. Egyptian culture still endured in building styles and the rulers were still seen as pharaohs, although various Egyptian and Greek gods were merged to become composite deities. Egypt would remain under the control of the Ptolemaic dynasty until it became a province of the Roman Empire after Octavian (the future Emperor Augustus) had defeated the Ptolemaic queen Cleopatra VII and her lover Mark Antony at the Battle of Actium in 31 BC.

Building a legend

Alexander began work on his new capital Alexandria the year after he seized power in Egypt, although he left the city after a few months and never returned there alive (he died in Babylon in 323 BC and his body was brought back to Alexandria, where his tomb became an object of pilgrimage).

With the Nile delta to the east, the deserts of Libya to the west and the protective island of Pharos just offshore, it was an ideal site for a new city. It took on the role later inherited by Venice – the main hub for trade between Europe and the East. It was also a strongly multicultural city, blending the cultures of Greece and Egypt as well as being home to what was then the largest Jewish community in the world. Being fabulously wealthy, it also became a powerful seat of learning and culture, exemplified by the city's famous library. Only Rome could surpass it in magnificence – a status that lasted until tensions between Greeks and Egyptians led to unrest and civil war. The city recovered something of its status under Roman rule, but in AD 641 fell to the Arabs.

Building a lighthouse

The Lighthouse of Alexandria was built between 280 and 247 BC by Ptolemy I, and finished by his son, Ptolemy II, records of its construction and magnificence handed down by historians such as Pliny the Elder and even Julius Caesar. It was sited on the little island of Pharos, now linked to the mainland by a mile-long 'mole', and acted as a guide for ships by marking the mouth of the city's harbour. Its beam was said to be visible 30 miles out to sea.

An image of the lighthouse appears on second-century coins, depicting a high, many tiered tower, with statues of Triton high up on the four corners of the top tier.

The lighthouse was said to be constructed from solid blocks of limestone resting on a base of red granite, the joints between the blocks sealed with lead or tar to make them more watertight. The light at the top was produced by an oil-powered furnace, the flame burning behind panes of glass.

The Lighthouse at Alexandria remained largely intact until AD 956, when it was badly damaged in an earthquake. Several subsequent earthquakes in the fourteenth century wrecked it further, and by the end of the fifteenth century so little was left that the ruling Sultan of Egypt built a fort on the site, recycling much of the Lighthouse's masonry in the process.

The Pharos of Abusir

About 30 miles from Alexandria lies the so-called Pharos of Abusir, a three-storey structure some 100 feet high, which is still extant and may well be a contemporary scaled-down model of the Lighthouse of Alexandria. Built as a funerary monument rather than a lighthouse, it does convey something of the Lighthouse's probable appearance, albeit in miniature.

Lighthouses from the Roman period do exist, although they're not classed as wonders of the world. There's a very fine example at La Coruña, Spain, and the remains of one at Dover Castle have been incorporated into the base of a watchtower.

Alexander the Great

He died at the age of 32, but by then through military brilliance, personal charisma and sheer force of will he'd already irrevocably changed the face of the Ancient World. He was Alexander the Great, the military commander, scholar, ruler and politician, creator of a vast empire stretching from Greece to the Himalayas and one of the most famous names of history.

Born in 356 BC in Pella, the ancient capital of Macedonia, Alexander was the son of King Phillip II of Macedon and his ambitious and scheming wife Olympias. Educated by no less than the great philosopher Aristotle, by the age of 16 Alexander was appointed regent of Macedon in his father's absence, suppressing Thracian rebellions and already displaying the military genius, recklessness and inspirational leadership that would be his hallmarks.

By the age of 20 Alexander had inherited a kingdom following Phillip's assassination and immediately set about reasserting Macedonia's power over Greece. His next target was even more ambitious: the mighty Persian Empire.

In 334 BC Alexander's armies crossed the Hellespont into Asia Minor, and his progress was astonishing. He first conquered Syria and then moved south into Egypt, taking cities such as Tyre and Jerusalem en route. In Egypt he founded the great coastal city of Alexandria and travelled into the deserts of Libya to consult the Oracle of the Siwa Oasis, who is said to have foretold Alexander's destiny and declared him the son of the deity Zeus-Amun. Finally, in a series of decisive battles, including key confrontations at Issus and Gaugamela, Alexander suffered not a single defeat as he took on the forces of the Persian king, Darius III.

By the age of 25 Alexander was not just king of Macedonia and leader of the Greeks but also the pharaoh of Egypt and King of Persia. But this was not enough. His goal was to reach "the ends of the world and the Great Outer Sea", and he spent the remaining years of his life expanding an empire that would eventually encompass some two million square miles and spread the culture of Greece as far east as India and as far south as Egypt.

Only the demands of his troops stopped him expanding his empire even further east. Forced to turn back, he died in 323 BC in Babylon, most probably from a fever. His body was transported to Alexandria, where it was laid to rest in a tomb that became an object of pilgrimage for the likes of Julius Caesar.

Described as "a strong, handsome commander with one eye dark as the night and one blue as the sky", Alexander's ambitions were fostered in childhood by his mother Olympias who instilled in him a sense of destiny. He was married twice, first to Roxana, the daughter of a Bactrian nobleman, and then to Stateira, daughter of King Darius III of Persia. He is said to have had two sons, one by Roxana, another by a mistress. But the closest relationship of his life was probably with his friend and bodyguard Hephaestion whose death in 324 BC left Alexander bereft and broken.

Chapter 9: The Superstructure

The measures of the pyramid

This is an Egyptologist Petrie who, in the XIX century, is the first to have drawn attention to the extraordinary precision achieved by [23] the ancient Egyptians. The four faces measure at their base:

230.454 m to the south, 230.253 m to the north, 230.357 m to the west and 230.394 m to the east. The error obtained for a perfect square is only twenty cm (only 4.4 cm according to Mark Lehner [24]). The average error on the right angles of the base is 0 ° 3′6″. The average error on the orientation along the four cardinal points is also 0 ° 3′6″. The base of the pyramid was leveled with an error of a few centimeters.

The seats and the covering

It is easier to describe the external aspect of the pyramid than the internal mass, the design of which is not certain. The tunnel, connecting the large gallery to the descent, still allows us to glimpse the masonry of the pyramid massif which is limited to a liberation of roughly squared limestone blocks. The stones of the great pyramid have varying dimensions depending on the height at which they are located. It would seem obvious to note that the closer one gets to the top of the pyramid, the more the height of the foundations decreases. However, this rule is not applicable here. The seats decrease in height to a certain level above the ground then, from this one increase in size until they decrease again and so on. There are thus eighteen groups with a variable number of seats. Egyptologist Georges Goyon explains this particularity by the origin and nature of the materials used, a limestone quarry whose subsoil is made up of strata of varying thicknesses. The pyramid is today composed of 201 seats with an average height of 0.69 meters, the last having disappeared and the top being reduced to a platform of a few hundred square meters. The pyramid, however, does not represent an entirely artificial volume. Egyptian indeed benefited from a rising rock on which they erected the body of the masonry. The limit

top of this eminence is clearly visible at the level of the cave. This peculiarity poses even more the problem of the extreme precision with which they accomplished the leveling of the base on its four sides.

The facing, originally composed of fine limestone from Tourah, has almost completely disappeared. He did

[25]

still more than a few blocks to the level of the base

Regarding the masonry, Petrie notes that:

, based on the stones of the base.

"Several measurements were made of the thickness of the joints between the facing stones. [26] The average thickness for those in the northeast is 0.002 inches and therefore the average error from the straight line and the perfect square is only 0.01 inch for a length of 75 inches on the height of the face. Although the stones had been brought within 1/50 inch of each other, in [27] other words in contact, the average opening of the joint was only 1/100 inch."

The notch and cavity of the northeast corner

A large notch is clearly visible in the northeast corner of the Great Pyramid. In 2008 and under the leadership of Jean-Pierre Houdin, the Egyptologist Bob Brier climbed to this platform in order to find clues in order to validate the theory of the French architect. For lack of convincing clues, Brier discovered to the east a cavity in the masonry. This is completely gone unnoticed in the eyes of Georges Goyon and Flinders Petrie, who methodically scrutinized in their time that part of the building. However, there is a (unique) mention of this cavity, in Journal of a Route across India and through Egypt to England in 1817-18 , travel reports written by Lieutenant-Colonel George Augustus Federick Fitzclarence and published in 1819. The

latter explored the site in the company of Giovanni Battista Belzoni and Henry Salt, and climbed alone the steps of the immense staircase formed by the foundations of the great pyramid. Here is his description :

"About two-thirds of my way up the northeast corner of the pyramid, I found a small cavity about twelve feet deep and twelve feet high, which appears to have been formed by removing the few large blocks. Stone. "

The pyramidion

There is no trace of the pyramidion that once crowned the top of the great pyramid. The pyramidion which is currently exposed near the south-eastern corner is none other than that of the small satellite pyramid. This one is in limestone and anepigraph, like the pyramidion of the red pyramid built by the father of Cheops, Snefrou. However, there is no clue to indicate any similarity with the disappeared pyramidion.

The apothem phenomenon

This phenomenon, which is encountered in other pyramids, is

[28]

very visible here

. The faces have a slight indentation in the

[29]

center, clearly visible when the sun is facing the pyramid. It was often invoked erosion or damage due to falling facing stones. It is also possible that the construction method is the origin. Indeed, Vito Maragioglio and Celeste Rinaldi noted that at the pyramid of Menkaure, this concavity disappeared at the level of the granite facing. IES Edwards attributes this peculiarity to the fact that the rock beds are slightly dumped towards the center of

[30]

each course, hence the depression. Currently, no satisfactory

explanation can explain this architectural feature already noticed

th

the XVIIIcentury.

Mathematical and astronomical considerations

When we study the geometry of the great pyramid, it is difficult to distinguish between the intentions of the builders and the properties which result from the proportions of the building. We often mention the golden ratio and the number pi inscribed in the proportions of the pyramid: the Egyptians indeed chose a slope, for the faces, of 14/11 (the height being 280 cubits and the base 2

× 220 cubits, the slope is equal to 280/220 = 14/11). This value was for the first time applied to the pyramid of

Meïdoum but is not a rule among the builders of the Old Kingdom since some pyramids have a slope of 6/5 (red pyramid), 4/3 (Khephren pyramid) or even 7/5 (rhomboidal pyramid).

• Regarding the golden ratio, the proportion of 14/11 leads to a report

apothem / half-base equal to, close to

[31]

• The value of the number would be given by the ratio (half-perimeter of the base) / height. We thus

[31]

obtain the approximate value.

These two results therefore follow from the use of a slope of 14/11. If this is to be seen as a deliberate desire to include them in the construction, the credit would go to the architect who for the first time used this slope at the pyramid of Meïdoum, completed during the reign of Snefrou.

There were many theories aimed at making the pyramid an astronomical observatory. Thus the descending corridor would

[32]

have pointed to the polar star of the time, Alpha Draconis.

The south side ventilation corridors would have pointed for one, the star Sirius, and for

the other, the star Alnitak. However, here again and as with most of the pyramids in Egypt, the access corridors had simple slopes that were easy to implement. They were inclined at an angle of between 26 ° and 26 ° 30 ', ie a slope of 1/2. However, a geometric property seems to have been desired by the architect of the great pyramid. The ventilation ducts for the queen's chamber would both reach the same level of the

[33]

pyramid. This fact is verified in the ducts of the king's chamber .

The supposed model

[34]

The underground passages are likened to a sketch (on a reduced scale) of the descent and the ascending corridor of the great pyramid. They are located at the northeast corner of the Great

[35]

Pyramid.

We recognize in these remains, the descent, a passage 21 meters long on a slope of 26 ° 32 'and whose section is 1.05 meters by 1.20. 11 meters from the entrance, a passage associated with the ascending corridor begins in the ceiling of the descent and joins the bottom of the large gallery which is outlined down to ground level. The section of the ascending corridor is wider than that of the descent to accommodate block caps. A vertical shaft of square section of 0.727 m, unparalleled in the large pyramid has been arranged to connect the outside to the first branch.

One of the main differences between the internal layout of the Great Pyramid and this infrastructure

is, in addition to that of proportions, the underground arrangement in the model of elements appearing in the body of the masonry of the great pyramid. In addition, the descent has not been dug in its entirety and the underground chamber is absent.

Although it is not accompanied by any superstructure, the Egyptologist Mark Lehner sees it as an unfinished burial. Despite the similarities in plan between the pyramid and this structure, the debate is still

[36]

not settled.

Construction of the pyramid of Cheops

The construction of the "great pyramid" began around -2650 (IV

Dynasty) and would have lasted about

twenty years according to the ancient historian Manetho (which seems plausible for modern Egyptologists). Many hypotheses have been proposed to explain the construction of the great pyramid. But none are definitely convincing.

Pseudo-scientific theories on the destination of the pyramid

The excessiveness and precision obtained at the great pyramid of Khufu seem, for some authors, incompatible with the knowledge and rudimentary means of the people who erected it. Several pseudo- scientific theses emerged, only very rarely inspired by archaeological data, to explain the destination of this monument. There were the proponents of the biblical thesis aiming to demonstrate that the great pyramid was erected by a people chosen by god, and the proponents of a superior civilization of Atlantean origin, even extraterrestrial.

Exploring the pyramid of ' Antiquity to the XIX

The first historians and travelers to tell us about their explorations are Greek and Latin authors: Herodotus,

Diodorus Siculus, Strabo, Pliny the Elder. Their descriptions are more focused on the historical and

legendary aspect that surrounds the monument than on the structure of the building itself. Herodotus, the first traveler whose writings have come down to us, mentions ideographic inscriptions on the faces of the

[37]

pyramid, detailing what it had cost in horseradish, onions and garlic for the workers (this surprising

indication is repeated by Diodorus). Only Strabo, in his Geography , cites a lifting door at the entrance to the pyramid, allowing access to the descent; but it doesn't say anything about internal distribution .

Later, many Arab authors relate the research of Caliph Al-Mamoun carried out in the great pyramid in the year 820. But the testimonies diverge. According to some, the caliph would have found nothing more than a

sarcophagus containing a corrupt body

. As the historian of X

century, Masudi says:

"We practiced for him the gap is still wide open today, was employed for this the fire, the vinegar, the levers ... The thickness of the wall was about twenty cubits; having reached the end of this wall, they found at the bottom of the hole a green basin filled with coined gold ; there it

[39] , [38]

was a thousand dinars each dinar weighing a once ... This basin was said, emerald   . "

The only problem with this description is that we know from a reliable source that the Egyptians did not know about currency.

th

The writer of the XIIcentury, Kaisi, wrote that Al-Mamun found there

" A square chamber at the base and vaulted at the top, very large and in the middle of which was dug a well ten cubits deep ... It is said that a man having entered there arrived at a small chamber where there was a statue of a man in green stone like malachite. This statue was brought to Al-Mamoun. It had a cover that was removed and the body of a man was found covered with a gold breastplate, encrusted with all kinds of precious stones ; on the chest was raised a sword of a price priceless, and close to the head was found a ruby red ... The statue where the dead had been shot was thrown close to the door of the government palace in Cairo,

[38]

where I saw it in the year 511 (1117-1118 of the Christian era)   . "

Many allusions to the characters engraved on the faces of the pyramid will be made until they deteriorate. According to Maçoudi, these characters were of several kinds; Greeks, Phoenicians and other unknowns.

[40]

These were undoubtedly testimonies engraved by travelers and accumulated over several centuries.

[41]

Ibn Khaldun reports in his Prolegomenathat the Caliph Al-Mamun would destroy the pyramids and

gathered the workers for this, but it n ' there succeeds not. His advisers then recommended him to leave them in place as a testimony to the greatness of the Arabs, since they had been able to defeat a civilization capable of creating such monuments. Part of the surface debris of the pyramids would have been used in the construction of some houses in Cairo, according to the statements collected by this same historian.

In the Middle Ages and at the beginning of the Renaissance, the pyramids were assimilated to Joseph's granaries, and few explorers gave a somewhat faithful description of the place. Not

th

until the middle of the XVIIcentury and the book

Pyramidographia John Greaves and finally see a detailed map of internal arrangements of the Great Pyramid. One discerns the ramp blocked at mid-term by a pile of debris, the room of the queen littered with rubble, the large gallery and the king's chamber. In 1754, the work of the historian Rollin edited by the English Knapton is illustrated with a view of the great gallery.

It was between the years 1798 and 1801 that the scientific mission commissioned by Vivant Denon during the Egyptian campaign was able to establish the first rigorously archaeological observations of the great pyramid. In addition to magnificent plates representing the site of Giza, the monumental Description of Egypt, published on the order of Emperor Napoleon Bonaparte, gives us the first realistic views of the interior of the great pyramid, as well as plans of very high precision. The publication of the description will cause a real craze. Travelers and explorers

will succeed during the XIXth century. Engineers Howard Vyse

and John Shae Perring will excavate, dig and leave many traces of their passages in most of the Memphite pyramids and more particularly in the large one.

Their results still provide valuable information today for those who want to study the Great Pyramid.

From this date, the great pyramid will be studied and measured in its smallest details by very many scientists, specialized or not in this discipline. Two books were then widely distributed: the very controversial Our Inheritance in the Great Pyramid , by Scottish astronomer Charles Piazzi

Smyth and The pyramids and temples of Giza, by Petrie.

Tourism related to the pyramid of Cheops

A major tourist spot, the pyramids are threatened by the rapid urbanization of the Giza plateau. As a result, a new policy for the protection of the plateau is being developed, in particular with the construction of a fence around its entire perimeter, thus delimiting the protected archaeological zone and the development of two separate entrances. Access for non-Egyptian tourists will be from the north of the site, precisely near the pyramid of Cheops.

The pyramid of Cheops and fiction

Comic

- Edgar P. Jacobs, The Mystery of the Great Pyramid (1954-1955), volumes 4 and 5 of the Blake and Mortimer series

- Lucien De Gieter, The talisman of the great pyramid, volume 21 of the adventures of Papyrus

Cinema

• Land of the Pharaohs by Howard Hawks, 1954

• 10,000 BC by Roland Emmerich, 2008

Esoteric literature

• The secret of the Great Pyramid by Georges Barbarin, I have read L'Aventure Mystérieuse n ° A216

Television

• In the television series Stargate SG-1, Dr. Daniel Jackson theorizes that the usefulness of pyramids such as the Great Pyramid of Cheops is to be the basis of landing for the vessels space alien of great size (of which the concavity responds to the convexity of the pyramids).

Related articles

• Cheops funeral complex (to which this pyramid belongs) ;

• Pyramids of Egypt ;

- Theories on the method of construction of the Egyptian pyramids .

A legend ?

The historical reality of these gardens is nowadays seriously questioned. In the XIX

century,

archaeologist H. Rassam gardens located north of the city near the palace outside. During the great German excavations , Robert Koldewey suggests that an arched construction of the south palace could have supported a terraced roof and thus correspond to the location of these famous gardens. In fact, no formal localization was found. That which adds to the doubt of archaeologists and the historians is that none of the documents cuneiform found on the website of Babylon will actually referring to these gardens.

It is in fact curious that a king like Nebuchadnezzar II who will cease to be congratulated for his

[2]

achievements (walls, gates, palaces, etc.) remains silent on these hypothetical gardens .

During the 1990s, the English Assyriologist Stéphanie Dalley put forward a hypothesis that seems more plausible, namely that the historians of antiquity confused Nineveh and Babylon. Indeed, no Babylonian source mentions the gardens, no classical Greek author alludes to them (Herodotus for example is completely silent on the subject). The only authors referring to it

are historians of the Hellenistic or Roman period, of whom they often

confuse the two capitals of the two empires preceding the Persian Empire. Finally the Assyrian rulers,

th

especially VIIcentury BC. AD, have gardens built in Nineveh. A text by Sennacherib thus evokes those

he had fitted out and describes the machines necessary for irrigation. A bas-relief from the palace of Ashurbanipal shows a hill covered with vegetation and supplied with water by an aqueduct and a system of canals. In addition, we know that, because of the embankment of the rivers, the irrigation had recourse to a system of "endless screw" which, by turning, raised the water to the level of the crops. The crops thus irrigated thus seemed to be suspended, or, in any case, clearly above the water level. Stéphanie Dalley concludes that the Hanging Gardens were therefore in Nineveh and not in Babylon. This explanation, although probable, is still under debate.

Appendices

Notes and references

[1] (en) [pdf] Karen Polinger Foster; "Gardens of Eden: Flora and Fauna in the Ancient Near East" (http: / / environment.yale.edu/documents/downloads/0-9/103foster.pdf); Transformations of Middle Eastern Natural Environments:

Legacies and Lessons ; New Haven ; Yale University ; 1998 ; pages 320-329

[2]   (en) Robin Fowler ; The Hanging Gardens of Babylon The Mysterious Wonder of the Ancient World

- Brigitte Lion, "In search of hanging gardens", Histoire magazine n ° 301 (September 2005).

- S. de Serdakowska, The Hanging Gardens of Semiramis , 1965.

Chryselephantine statue of Olympian Zeus

Chryselephantine statue of Olympian Zeus

→ Wonders of the world

A fanciful representation of the statue of Zeus, engraving by Philippe Galle in 1572, from a sketch by Maarten van

Heemskerck

Longitude latitude   37 ° 63 ' 78 " North 21 ° 63 ' 00 " East

Country Greece

City Olympia

Construction date it. -432

Construction time

Main materials gold and ivory

Builder Phidias

Utility religious

Date of destruction 462

Cause of destruction fire

The chryselephantine statue of Olympian Zeus is a work of the Athenian sculptor Phidias, made around 436 BC. AD in Olympia. Now extinct, it was considered in Antiquity as the third of the → seven wonders of the world.

Description

According to Pausanias

, the statue shows Zeus sitting on his throne, representation which goes back to

the Iliad and spreading in Greek art from the VI

- it seems, moreover, that the sculptor

was deliberately inspired by Homer. The god is crowned with an olive branch. In his right hand, he holds

a statuette of Nike, personification of victory, itself represented crowned with a headband and a garland.

We do not know its proportions. In his left hand, Zeus holds a richly decorated scepter, on which an eagle is perched. The god is draped in a himation (mantle) embroidered with animal figures and flowers, and wears sandals. His throne has a decoration that is both carved, inlaid (precious stones, ebony) and painted. Four small dancing Victories crown the feet of the throne, and two other Victories appear at its base.

The set is made using the chryselephantine technique: plates of gold (χρυσός / khrusós) and ivory (ελεφάντος / elephántos) cover a wooden core and respectively represent, on the one hand, the hair, the beard, the sandals and drapery, on the other hand the bare parts (in particular the skin). It is about 12 meters high, including 1 meter for the base and 2 meters for the pedestal. A kalos inscription on one of the fingers, "Pantarkès is beautiful ", allows the statue to be dated approximately : the so- called Pantarkès won in 436 BC. AD the boys' wrestling event at the Olympic Games.

The statue enjoys great fame throughout the entire Greek world. It is included in the → Seven Wonders of the World list. By reverence for the sculptor's workshop where he carves the giant with his students is kept

. At the same time, the statue is

removed from the temple and will join, in Constantinople, the prodigious collection of Lausos, chamberlain

[3]

of Theodosius II, which includes among others the Aphrodite of Cnidus

. She disappeared in a fire in

461, at the same time as the other statues. Unfortunately, no copy in marble or in bronze is reached to

us. In contrast, the work of Phidias has been identified with more or less certainty on a series of Roman

[4]

coins minted from 98 to 198 AD. AD

Posterity and influence

The abbot Barthélémy in Voyage of the young Anacharsis in Greece, towards the middle of the fourth century before the vulgar era (1843), writes that "the Jupiter of Olympia will always serve as a model for artists who want to represent the Supreme Being with dignity. "

The statue is at the origin of the representation of Christ Pantocrator in Byzantine art. She inspired

Daniel Chester French for his portrayal of Abraham Lincoln at the Lincoln Memorial and Salvador Dalí, in his painting The Statue of Zeus, in Olympia painted in 1954.

Temple of Artemis at Ephesus

Temple of Artemis at Ephesus

→ Wonders of the world

Temple ruins

Longitude latitude   37 ° 56 ′ 59 ″ North 27 ° 21 ′ 50 ″ East

Country   Turkey

City   Ephesus

Construction date   -560

Construction time   120 years

Main materials   Pierre

Builder   Theodore of Samos, Ctesiphon, Metagenes

Utility religious

Date of destruction   July 21 -356

Cause of destruction   arson

The temple of Artemis at Ephesus (in Greek Ἀρτεμίσιον / Artemísion , in Latin Artemisium) is in Antiquity one of the most important sanctuaries of Artemis, Greek goddess of hunting and wild nature.

On the site of an older sanctuary, a temple was built around 560 BC. AD by Theodore of Samos, Ctesiphon and Metagenes and funded by King Croesus of Lydia. Its colossal dimensions and the richness of its decoration explain its mention in 16 of the 24 lists of the → Seven wonders of the world which have come

[1]

down to us

. It was burnt down on purpose in 356 BC. BC by Erostrate, who wants to make himself

th

famous by destroying the temple. A second temple is built in the middle of the IV century BC. AD on the

same plan. It was looted by the Ostrogoths in 263 and then burned by the Christians in 401. Justinian finished dismantling it by removing part of its columns for the imperial palace of Constantinople.

The ruins of Ephesus are found today near of the city Turkish of Selçuk, at fifty kilometers south of Izmir.

This temple is also regarded as being the first bank in the world because it was possible for there drop of money and of the recover more later credited with an interest.

History

Location

The website sacred to Ephesus is much more older than the 'Artemision . Pausanias the Periegetes

[2]

described in IIcentury BC. AD, the sanctuary of Artemis as very old. He says with certainty that it is well

before the time of ion migration in the region of Ephesus, and more ancient even than the sanctuary of the oracle of Apollo at Didyma. He says that people pre-ionic of the city were Leleges and Lydian. This version was confirmed in 1908 by excavations carried out by DG Hogarth which made it possible to identify three successive temples built on the same site as the temple of Artemis in Ephesus. Seconds excavations in

1987-1988 have also confirmed the release that gives Pausianas the previous story building the temple of Ephesus. Callimachus, in his Hymn to

Artemis, attributes the origin of the temenos of Ephesus to the

[3]

Amazons, of which he already imagines a cult centered on an icon (Bretas) :

" The warlike Amazons t ' rose, formerly a statue on the shore of ' Ephesus, at the foot of the trunk of ' beech; HIPPO performs rites and Amazons, Queen Oupis around your image danced to ' first armed dance, dance shields, and then developed in a circle their large chorus; [...] Around this statue, later, a vast sanctuary was built; daylight never n ' in illuminated more worthy of the gods or most opulent [...] "

- Callimachus, Hymns III to Artemis c. 237-250

The Ephesus site is occupied since the Bronze Age, and the first temple built on the very site of the temple

of Ephesus was in the second half of the VIII

. This first peripteral temple in Ephesus is the oldest example of a peripteral temple on the coast of Asia Minor, and possibly the oldest Greek-style temple surrounded by colonnades.

destroyed the temple and deposited more than half a meter of sand on the site. Bammer notes that although the site is flooded and has been raised by nearly two meters th e century BC. The site was retained, which he said means "that maintaining the identity of the actual site plays an important role in sacred organization" (Bammer 1990: 144). According to Pliny the Elder, on the other hand, the site was selected for its marshy nature, as a precaution against earthquakes, and not because of the age of worship [6] on the site.

The archaic temple

The new temple, built in marble, with a double row of peripteral columns leaving room for a wide ceremonial passage around the cella, was designed and built around -550 by the Cretan architects Chersiphron and his son Metagenes. A new cult statue in ebony is carved by Endoios, the previous one

[7]

having been probably destroyed in the flood, and a naiskos to shelter it is erected east of the altar in the

open air. This reconstruction was financed by Croesus, the wealthy king of Lydia.

The temple attracted many merchants, kings, and the curious, as well as many devotees of the cult of Artemis , many of whom paid homage, to Artemis in the form of jewelry and various merchandise. It found what could be the oldest pieces of electrum (an alloy gold-silver) as well as of many other objects of value.

This temple was

also highly respected as a place of refuge, a tradition linked to the myth of the Amazons, who would have taken refuge on the site of the temple in front of Heracles and Dionysus.

Hellenistic temple

The temple was burned down on July 21 -356 by Erostrate, who wanted to make himself famous

Learning the motive of the arsonist who had destroyed the temple which was the envy of all the Greeks, the magistrates of the city had him tortured and killed. His name was forbidden to be pronounced on pain of death. This judgment was only respected for 23 years, until the arrival of Alexander the Great, who offered

[8]

to finance the restoration of the temple. When the Ephesians learned of their benefactor's date of birth (the same night as the fatal fire), Erostratus's name was revealed. Fearing that Alexander's triumph would be short-lived, the Ephesians diplomatically refused, explaining that it was not proper for a god to dedicate one temple to another. The reconstruction was therefore financed by several cities to which Artemision acted as a bank.

Deprived of some of his most famous works of art by Nero, looted by an expedition of Goths from the Black Sea around 262, damaged by earthquakes, the temple was permanently closed, like other pagan temples, by the general edict of Theodosius in 381. The temple is mentioned in the Acts of the Apostles (XIX : 23-40) in particular for the riot that the preaching of Paul of Tarsus started there .

[1]

In 401, the temple was finally destroyed by a crowd led by Saint John Chrysostom , and the stones

were used in the construction of other buildings. Some of the columns of Hagia Sophia originally belonged

to the Temple of Artemis.

Rediscovery

After six years of patient research, the temple site was rediscovered in 1869 by an expedition sponsored by

[16]

the British Museum, led by John Turtle Woodand although several artefacts and sculptures have been found, it remains today only one column of the temple proper.

A British traveler, Edward Falkener, stayed in Asia Minor in 1844-1845 and spent two weeks in Ephesus. It is made a survey of all the ruins he saw, attempting to reconstruct a map of the city. He published his hypotheses in 1862. He had identified (with reason) the ruins in the valley between Mount Pion and Mount Coressus as those of the Porte de Magnesia. He then guess is (quite rightly) that the temple was to be

[17]

found in the alignment of the door.

The architect and engineer English John Turtle Wood had been commissioned in 1858 by the Ottoman Empire for the construction of the railway stations of Smyrn e to Ayd ı n . Su r up , i l s e passionate has lice r the search of the temple of Artemis at Ephesus. He had no specific qualifications other than his enthusiasm. In 1863, he had obtained that the British ambassador in Constantinople negotiate a irman authorizing him to undertake excavations, but also to export all the antiques.

[18]

that he would find. In Turkey since 1858 Wood had not read the book of Falkener, but

he had put forward a fairly similar hypothesis: succeed in identifying a monument in order to then conjecture the position of the temple. He also considered, as an architect, as Chersiphron had had to

[17]

choose a tray little high, as it is located in the west of the city to install its building . In spring 1863, he

hired five workers who had been laid off from his construction of road from iron to check its assumptions. He continued, however, to reside in Smyrna, rather than on site. Also, it would make the return journey all the days. He had a hour and a half of walking between his home and the station then three and a half hour train to cover the eighty kilometers from Smyrna to Ayasoluk.

He dug with his men for five to six hours and the more hot the day before starting the return trip. In June, his workers refused to continue the excavations during the summer. He failed to convince them. Work resumed in September. It was then rented an apartment in Ayasoluk, in a such a state of disrepair that it did not have to pay rent. He explored the surroundings of the Great Gymnasium, which his main source Richard Chandler considered to be the temple. He dug as the level of the ancient port. It seems he has dug a little to chance. He only put a few inscriptions up to date

. He had thus dug at his own expense seventy-five rather deep holes on the plateau

[18]

southwest of Ayasoluk.

In early 1864 he turned to the British Museum to which he wrote to ask for £ 100 in funding . His letter

was well received: Charles Newton, the curator of the Department of Greek and Roman Antiquities at the British Museum, had discovered the

→ Mausoleum at Halicarnassus in somewhat similar conditions when he was Vice-Consul of Great Britain in Lesbos. He therefore did not take a negative view of this approach. Moreover, that an agent of the British

[19]

Museum discovered a second Wonder of the World was not to displease its directors .

Wood got his funding. As work resumed on the track, he returned to Smyrna and do could be make on the site all the days. He had hired a foreman who supervised about forty workers. They cleared the odeon under more than ten meters of earth. Numerous registrations were updated. However, this will suit not to Wood who will desire that the temple. He spent his evenings with his wife reconstructing the puzzles of the inscriptions, hoping to find clues. He began to become famous and the guest inscribed the site of

[20]

excavations from the stages of their journey. He was even the victim of an assassination attempt.

From 1866 to 1868, thanks to a new advance from the British Museum, Wood had the theater area

searched . In 1868, his findings were embarked on the HMS Terrible . The museum's investment was paying off. However, the difficulties began to accumulate. In case of the malaria endemic in the marshes around the site, the health of Wood deteriorated. He returned to England in the summer of 1867. He had problems recruiting since that of its workers had been murdered and all the other stopped the investigation of time that does not succeed. He was the victim of new assassination attempts. The brigands attacked his site.

He fell into one of his holes. Local farmers protested against these same holes that rendered their lands unsuitable for the crop and they demanded an increase of compensations financial. The application of more high was for £

50 that Wood managed to bring in £ 3. Finally, his inscription stamps were attacked by

[20]

mice.

The 1867 theater campaign, however, uncovered an inscription concerning the gold and silver statuettes donated to the temple by the wealthy Roman C. Vibius Salutaris. She described the statuettes and their route from the city to the temple through the Magnesia Gate. Using this door to find the temple had been Falkener's idea. The entire 1868 season was devoted to clearing the road. After about forty meters, he came to a fork. Wood continued to clear the two branches towards Magnesia and towards Ayasoluk. There, after 150 meters, he discovered the stoa that Philostratus said was 600 feet. At the end of May, running out

[21]

of money, he suspended the work and returned to England.

The British Museum renewed its trust and funding in him. The 1869 campaign progressed nearly a kilometer towards Ayasoluk. Tombs, including that of Androclus, were put to day. At the foot of the hill Ayasoluk, a road off of five meters and lined with white marble sarcophagi was released. The excavations had to be interrupted because the peasants refused that their fields of barley, almost ripe, be touched.

Wood decided to take on an olive grove, but his irman had expired. He made a quick return to Constantinople and succeeded in the renewal. When his workers dug between the olive trees, they extricated a thick wall of stone very

massive bearing Latin and Greek inscriptions testifying to its construction by Emperor Augustus in AD 6. However, they refused to dig any further without payment and Wood's funds were exhausted. He obtained

an extension from the British Museum which specified that it would be the last if the temple was not

[21]

discovered.

Wood finally found the remains of the temple on December 31, 1869, six meters below the surface. He cleared first the marble pavement, then the foundations of the archaic temple. He published a first account of his discoveries in 1877. DG Hogarth and

AE Henderson opened a new excavation campaign in 1905-1905. They were able to unearth the remains of three previous temples which they named A, B and C, the temple of Croesus taking the letter D. The site has been excavated since 1965 by the Institute of Archeology in Vienna.

, whose account is confused and does not

. According to him, the temple is 225 feet by

425 feet and has 127 columns 60 feet high; 36 of them are carved in relief (columnæ cælatæ), including one by Scopas. Unfortunately, we do

not know the measurement of the foot to which Pliny refers; the odd number of columns is also a source of query. Vitruvius describes a dipterous temple, that is to say surrounded by a double row of columns, with eight columns on each of the short sides. Finally, Philo of Byzantium indicates that the temple is on a podium of 10 steps.

The sculptures of the archaic temple

Only a few fragments of the frieze have survived from the abundant relief decoration which adorned both the lower drums of the columns and the parapet. The subject of the decoration of the columns seems to have been a procession: some of the figures, represented on the march, seem to carry a basket or other offering; the fragments also show cattle and horses. The carved decoration of the parapet probably had

several different subjects: a procession of chariots and horses, a fight of armed men, Amazons, animals,

etc.

. As it stands, the fragments only allow us to say that the sculptures were in keeping with the style

[28]

of central and northern Ionia smile .

: shape of the head, soft contours of the face, full nostrils and lips, slight

The sculptures of the later temple

Several of the sculpted columns of the later temple have been found; they are currently kept in the British Museum.

[29]

Only one of them is in good condition. It represents a naked

winged young man who, if it were not for his sword, could be an Eros. Another naked young man, wearing a cloak over his arm, is easily recognized as Hermes thanks to the caduceus he holds in his right hand. The two young people are surrounded by women wearing peplos; a very mutilated male figure is shown seated and wears elaborately designed sandals.

Its subject has not been identified with certainty: a representation of Heracles before Aaque, a competition of Muses, who would be collectively embodied by the young winged man, or an episode of

the myth of Pandora

. The most plausible hypothesis

[29]

is a

representation of the myth of Alceste, who volunteered to die in place of her husband Admetus. The winged young man would therefore be Thanatos, personification of death, which Euripides stages in the prologue to his tragedy Alceste : Thanatos arrives armed with a sword with which he will cut a lock of Alceste's hair, just as the 'officiant of a sacrifice cuts a tuft of hair on the head of the animal he is going

[31]

immolate. Here, Thanatos would entrust to Hermès, in his role of psychopompe (conductor

souls), the soul of Alceste; one of the women, standing and holding a wedding crown, would be Persephone; the seated male figure would be Hades on his throne.

Mausoleum of Halicarnassus

Mausoleum of Halicarnassus

→ Wonders of the world

Representation by the Dutch artist Maarten van Heemskerck of the Mausoleum at Halicarnassus

Longitude latitude   37 ° 02 ' 16.6 " North 27 ° 25 ' 26.6 " East

Country   Turkey

City   Bodrum

Construction date   from -353 to -350

Construction time   3 years

Main materials   marble

Builder   Satyrus, Pythis

Utility religious

Date of destruction   thth

XIIIand XIVcenturies

Cause of destruction   multiple earthquakes

The Mausoleum of Halicarnassus (Greek Μαυσωλεῖο ν / mausoleum ῖ is) es t s e tomb of Mausolus, king of Caria (Asia Minor), who died in

353 BC. AD). It was the fifth of the → Seven Wonders of the World. The monument was admired from Antiquity for its dimensions and its decoration, so much so that any large tomb , for example the mausoleum of the Emperor Hadrian, current Castel Sant'Angelo , is called a "mausoleum" . The mausoleum was located in the city of Bodrum (southwestern Turkey).

The Caria was a province dependent of the Empire Persian, but which had become almost autonomous. This is the king Mausolus who moved the capital to Halicarnassus, after having taken control of most of southwest Anatolia. Although officially dependent on the Persian Empire, it was of Greek culture. He undertook major works to embellish and fortify his capital. In particular, he had a theater and a temple built in Ares, the god of war.

Construction

According to tradition (Strabo, Pausanias), it was his sister and widow, Artémise II, who decided to build an exceptional monument in her honor.

However, as she did not reign until two years after him, it is probable that the monument was started during Mausole's very lifetime. It was completed in 350 BC. AD is one year after the death of Artemisia II. We do not know by whom it was completed, perhaps by Mausole's brother, perhaps by Alexander the Great, perhaps it was never even completed.

[1]

The building was said to have been designed by Pythéos de Priene

. The greatest contemporary artists

[2]

were required for the construction of the Mausoleum: according to Vitruvius

, Praxiteles would have

[3]

participated in it, alongside Léocharès, Bryaxis and Scopas, but this mention is considered doubtful .

The Mausoleum rested on a rectangular substruction, surrounded by a sacred enclosure (τέμενος / temenos) open to the east by a propylaea. The substructure was topped 36colonnes, supporting a pyramid of 24degrés, the summit of which is found a chariot marble.

He remained in good condition until the XII

thth

century and lack of maintenance, it fell into ruin. In the XV

century, the Hospitallers used it as a career to build the castle Saint-Pierre on the ancient acropolis of Halicarnassus, and to repair the city walls.

Archaeological discovery

In 1857 Charles Thomas Newton LOCA first the monument thanks to his knowledge of ancient literature, especially Vitruvius and Pliny the Elder, but also thanks to a mastery of the interpretation of fragments found on the ground, usually gained through a long work in the field.

He had to adapt his excavation technique to local conditions. Indeed, he did not have the means to buy all the land supposed to contain the Mausoleum. He therefore resorted to tunnels, not trenches, to locate the outer limits of the building. He could thus after having discovered the four corners buy only the fields which he wished to explore more in depth.

He removed from the ground many fragments of architecture and sculpture, including four slabs from the eastern frieze, a work by Scopas representing a fight between Greeks and Amazons. All these fragments, as well as one of the monumental wheels of the quadriga on which were the colossal statues of Mausole and Artemisia are in the British Museum. He was also able to collect in this museum the other identified fragments of the Mausoleum scattered in Geneva, Constantinople or Rhodes. There, his work as a curator joined that of an archaeologist.

See as well

Related articles

- Halicarnassus
- Mausolus
- Artemisia II
- Château Saint-Pierre

References

[1]   Martinez, The works attributed to Praxiteles, p. 43.

[2]   Vitruvius, Architecture (VII, pref., 13).

[3]   Muller-Dufeu the class in the category " works uncertain or attributed falsely to Praxiteles ," p. 517 ; Pasquier, "Elements of biography", p. 20 and "Praxiteles today? The question of the originals ", p. 83-84; Ridgway, p. 265. See the article Praxiteles for these references.

Colossus of Rhodes

Colossus of Rhodes

→ Wonders of the world

The Colossus of Rhodes as depicted in The Book of Knowledge (1911)

Longitude latitude   36 ° 27 ′ 04 ″ North 28 ° 13 ′ 40 ″ East

Country   Greece

City   Rhodes

Construction date   Around -292

Construction time   About 12 years

Main materials   Bronze

Builder   Hellenistic Greece

Utility Monument

Date of destruction   -227

Cause of destruction   Earthquake

The Colossus of Rhodes was a statue of Helios, in bronze, of which the height exceeded thirty meters, the work of Chares. Remembrance of the

st

resistance victorious Demetrius IPoliorcetes

(-305 to -304), built on the island of Rhodes to

-292, this gigantic effigy was overturned in -226 by an earthquake. Broken at the knees, she collapsed and fell to pieces. The broken statue remained in place until 654. Today, there is no longer the slightest trace of the colossus. It was the sixth of the → Seven Wonders of the Ancient World

.

The construction was long and laborious. The colossus was made entirely of wood and bronze. He took first be a soul in wood. One time the " skeleton " made in

instead, the structure was covered with huge bronze plaques. The foundry of the island enough not to take the needs of such business, the bronze was imported in

large quantity.

One spot traditionally the statue of Colossus on the great harbor of Rhodes, where it would have served to " door entry " (as it suggests the engraving below against). Now, after the static studies British specialists the statue could be on the harbor in the position that he attributed, in reason of the gap too large that suggests one such position. In fact, the pillars on which have rested the feet of the statue would have been separated a quarantine of meters, according to the observations of funds sailors in the bay of Rhodes conducted by these researchers. The difference thus observed would therefore not correspond to the height of the statue, which had to be slightly smaller than the Statue of Liberty in New York. In practice, this would have resulted in a distortion between the load and the support points of the statue.

The hypothesis that appeared during the Renaissance of a statue with legs apart and allowing boats to pass under it has therefore fallen into disuse. Today other avenues are being explored :

• One of them wants the statue to be on the heights of the island (or below the acropolis), thus overlooking the whole archipelago, thus giving a particular majesty to Helios and conferring on the statue a superhuman dimension .

• Another theory advocated among others by German architect and archaeologist Wolfram Hoepfner up the Colossus of Rhodes to the ' entry of the ' other harbor of Rhodes : the military port. According to Hoepfner the Colossus of Rhodes featured a "Saluting Helios" with his right hand .

The colossus was brought down by an earthquake around -225 / -227. Technically, the earthquake twisted the statue's knees. The pile of wood and copper thus formed, was, at first, left on the spot, because the oracle of Delphi would have forbidden the inhabitants to straighten the statue. Around 654, an Arab expedition took the 20 tons that remained of the colossus (13 tons of bronze and 7 tons of iron), to sell them to a Jewish merchant. The fact that the statue is made of wood and covered with bronze and, therefore, that it overlooks the entrance to the port, divides some historians. Indeed, it is difficult to imagine that a work of such weight rests solely on a wooden skeleton. So it had to be made of stone, and building a statue of this size is almost impossible.

In popular culture

• The story of the Colossus of Rhado inspired Sergio Leone to film The Colossus of Rhodes

released in 1961 with Lea Massari and Georges Marchal.

• The Colossus of Rhodes was also inspired Dali, in his painting "The Colossus of Rhodes" painted in 1954.

• The Colossus of Rhodes is a major enemy of the video game God of War II , released in 2007.

• The Colossus of Rhodes is destroyed by falling on a Kraken at the start of the video game Titan Quest: Immortal Throne, an expansion of the video game Titan Quest.

• The Colossus of Rhodes is one of the marvels of the Civilization IV video game to improve maritime resources .

- The Colossus of Rhodes is one of the wonders of the Rise of Nations video game . The wonder of the game, however, does not share a resemblance to the gods Helios

- In the Age of Mythology game, the player can build a colossus.

See as well

Bibliography

- Lawrence Durrell, Venus and the Sea , LGF-Livre de Poche, 1993.

- (de) Wolfram Hoepfner, Der Koloss von Rhodos , Publisher Philipp von Zabern, Mainz am Rhein, 2003.

Conclusion

I hope this book was able to help you inspire children about the 7 wonders of the ancient world.

The next step is to teach these kids that these 7 ancient wonders once existed and therefore they are not to be forgotten. They carry a tremendous cultural significance and the knowledge about them allows us to better understand ancient civilizations.

Thank you and good luck!

www.ingramcontent.com/pod-product-compliance
Lightning Source LLC
Chambersburg PA
CBHW050359120526
44590CB00015B/1755